A SIMPLIFIED GUIDE TO BHS*

CRITICAL APPARATUS, MASORA, ACCENTS UNUSUAL LETTERS & OTHER MARKINGS

Third Edition

William R. Scott

Also in this cover:

An English Key to the Latin Words and Abbreviations and the Symbols of Biblia Hebraica Stuttgartensia

by H. P. Rüger

Biblia Hebraica Stuttgartensia

Second Edition January 1990
Third Edition May 1995

An English Key to the Latin Words and the Symbols of Biblia Hebraica Stuttgartensia, by H. P. Rüger, is published in Stuttgart by the German Bible Society (1985) and is reprinted by arrangement with the United Bible Societies.

Library of Congress Cataloging-in-Publication Data
A Simplified Guide to BHS: Critical Apparatus, Masora, Accents, Unusual Letters & Other Markings / William R. Scott. — 3rd ed.
p. cm.
English, Hebrew, Aramaic, and Latin.
"Also in this cover: An English Key to the Latin Words and Abbreviations and the Symbols of Biblia Hebraica Stuttgartensia by H.P. Rüger."
Includes bibliographical references.
ISBN 0-941037-35-5
1. Biblia Hebraica Stuttgartensia. 2. Bible. O.T.—Criticism, Textual. I. Rüger, Hans Peter. English Key to the Latin Words and Abbreviations and the Symbols of Biblia Hebraica Stuttgartensia. II. Bible. O.T. Hebrew. 1977. III. Title.
BS7151977e 221.4'4—dc20 95-18818
CIP

Published by BIBAL Press
P.O. Box 821653
N. Richland Hills, TX 76182

CONTENTS

Preface v

Chapter 1. **The Divisions**
- Sôp̄ Pāsûq 1
- Paragraph Markings (Petûḥāʾ & Setûmāʾ) 1
- Sēder 1
- Pārāšāh 2

Chapter 2. **Special Points, Unusual Letters and Other Marks**
- Puncta Extraordinaria (Special Points) 3
- Unusual Letters
  - Inverted Nûn 3
  - Large Letters 4
  - Small Letters 4
  - Raised Letters 4
- Other Marks
  - Pasēq 5
  - Maqqēp̄ 5
  - Metheg 6
  - Rāp̄eh 7

Chapter 3. **Masora**
- The Masoretes 8
- Masora Finalis 10
- Masora Marginalis 11
- Masora Parva (Mp) 11
- Associating Mp Notes to the Text 12
- Qerê and Ketîb 13
- Perpetual Qerê 13
- Unique Words and Phrases 14
- Hebrew Numbers 14
  - Translating Mp 15
  - Seberin 15
  - Tiqqune Sopherim 15
  - Itture Sopherim 15
- Masora Magna (Mm) 16

Chapter 4. **BHS Critical Apparatus**
Relationship of the Text to Manuscripts 18
Associating Entries to the Text 19
Translating the Symbols 20
Value Judgements in Text Criticism 22
Translating Abbreviations and Latin 22

Chapter 5. **The Accents**
General 25
The Accents of the Twenty-One Books 27
The Accents of the Three Books 32
Cantillation 35

Chapter 6. **Index of Symbols and Abbreviations of the Small Masora** 37

Chapter 7. **Transliteration of Names and Terms** 52

Abbreviated Bibliography 57

Index 59

An English Key to the Latin Words and Abbreviations and the Symbols of Biblia Hebraica Stuttgartensia by H. P. Rüger 61

Table of Hebrew Numbers back cover

PREFACE

Armed with a beginning knowledge of Hebrew and some instruction on how to use a lexicon, I first opened the pages of BHS with great anticipation and was immediately dismayed to find an array of marks, symbols, and strange entries for which none of my texts had prepared me. I was then astonished to discover that the prefatory information in BHS simply did not offer satisfactory explanations of how to decipher them. After time-consuming research and with the help of several patient instructors, I eventually began to understand how to read and use this important information; but I never overcame the conviction that the learning process was more difficult than it needed to be. For Hebrew scholars, this may only be a transitory annoyance, but surely the vast majority of students, pastors, and other exegetes will appreciate simple instructions, gathered into a single source, which provide basic guidelines for understanding the critical apparatus, masora, accents, and other marks and symbols to be found in BHS. This little guide, then, makes no pretense to be either exhaustive or authoritative. Its sole purpose is to simplify one's initial attempts to fully utilize BHS.

This guide is designed to be used as a ready reference while reading BHS. For this reason, its contents are organized so as to facilitate ease of reference, rather than with the logic of an introductory text. If you are not already familiar with BHS, I recommend that you first read pages 8–10 and 18–19 before proceeding on to other sections.

For the beginning student, one of the most distressing features of the study of biblical Hebrew is the diversity of names and terms that appear to be used by different scholars. This is sometimes due to the alternative use of Hebrew or Aramaic words of similar meaning. Even when the same Hebrew or Aramaic names are used, variations result from differing methods of transliterating them or sometimes from the use of modern day Hebrew names. Not infrequently, these differences can be traced back to medieval or even ancient times. This array of choices forced difficult decisions in the printing of a guide such as this that attempts to be useful both to the beginner and to the experienced reader of BHS. The desirability of using simple, modern-looking terms free of transliteration symbols (which might simplify one's initial efforts), the fact that Jewish and Christian circles commonly spell terms quite differently, and the need to maintain traditional academic standards all had to be weighed against each other. The final decision (which will probably not quite satisfy anyone) was to use in nearly every case the system of transliteration and the spelling of names of Hebrew letters and vowels found in Thomas Lambdin's *Introduction to Biblical Hebrew*. Lambdin's transliteration has the advantage of allowing one to accurately reproduce the Hebrew or Aramaic name that lies behind the diversity of English renderings. Even so, a few terms are so nearly universally agreed upon that I have not used Lambdin's transliteration for them. Among these are: *dagesh* (although Lambdin and others use *daghesh*), *metheg*, *sopherim*, *seberin*, *itture*, *tiqqune*, and the names of the verb conjugations (*piel*, *hiphil*, etc.). Once the student becomes familiar with the transliteration symbols, various spellings are normally not so great as to create confusion. However, in a few cases, I have provided alternative spellings within the text of this guide in order to minimize uncertainty on the part of beginning students. In addition, chapter 7 was added a few scant days before publication in order to further reduce the amount of research that the conscientious novice might feel compelled to undertake simply to understand basic concepts. The list of alternative spellings and terms from chapter 7 is not intended to be comprehensive, but simply represents a characteristic sampling of forms encountered in the writing of this guide.

Numerous resources are available that provide detailed discussions of BHS apparatus, masora, and principles of textual criticism. Both Würthwein and Wonneberger provide excellent bibliographies. A few other useful references for further study are listed in the abbreviated bibliography at the end of this guide.

I would like to express my appreciation to Paul Brassey, Dr. Carl Graesser, Dr. Michael Guinan and Dr. Duane Christensen for their kind assistance in reviewing and suggesting improvements to this guide. In addition, a special word of thanks is due to Dr. Graesser, under whom I first studied intermediate Hebrew, and who gave his gracious permission to include in this booklet many of the words that I first heard in his classroom. My gratitude for all this assistance, however, in no way alters the fact that I am solely responsible for any errors.

ADDENDUM FOR THE FOURTH PRINTING

The author wishes to express his most sincere appreciation to the United Bible Societies for their gracious permission to reprint Rüger's English Key along with this guide, thus bringing under one cover all of the basic reference material that English-speaking students need in order to utilize all of the information printed in BHS.

ADDENDUM FOR THE THIRD EDITION

This book is dedicated to the memory of Dr. Carl Graesser.

1
THE DIVISIONS

SÔP̄ PĀSÛQ [:]

A large colon following a word signifies the end of a verse. This sign is called *sôp̄ pāsûq*, which means "end of verse." The end of a verse may or may not be the end of a sentence.

PARAGRAPH MARKINGS [Pᵉṯûḥāʾ and Sᵉṯûmāʾ]

At one time there was a significant difference between an "open" paragraph (one starting on a new line) and a "closed" paragraph (which started on the same line as the preceding paragraph with a short space separating the two). In many manuscripts, a פ or ס was put in front of each paragraph to preserve the distinction. The פ is an abbreviation for *pᵉṯûḥāʾ*, which means "open" and the ס is an abbreviation for *sᵉṯûmāʾ*, which means "closed." Over the years, increasing inconsistency developed concerning this difference in format, and it was largely ignored by the time of Codex Leningradensis, which does not mark the paragraphs with פ or ס. These marks are added by the editors of BHS. The entire Hebrew Bible (except for Psalms) is so divided.

SĒDER [ס̈]

This sign divides the Hebrew Bible into 452 lessons. These divisions are associated with the Palestinian tradition. They far predate the division into chapters, which was not made until the fourteenth century. The exact location of the divisions and their number vary somewhat among manuscripts. The masora at the end of the Pentateuch in BHS indicates that it contains 167 *sᵉdārîm*. Indeed if the number of *sᵉdārîm* listed in the masora following each of the five books (see pp. 10–11) are added up, they total 167. However, if one counts carefully, thirty-two *sᵉdārîm* can be discovered in Deuteronomy rather than the thirty-one listed. (The unnumbered one precedes chapter 20.) Thus, one can find 168 *sᵉdārîm* in the BHS Pentateuch. Whatever the proper number is, the *sᵉdārîm* were used as weekly liturgical readings or lessons that would cover the entire Pentateuch in about three years.

PĀRĀŠĀH [פרש]

These abbreviations divide the Pentateuch into fifty-four lessons. The *pārāšôṯ* are longer sections similar in function to the *sᵉdārîm*. However, they are associated with the Babylonian tradition. They appear only in the Pentateuch and provide for a one-year liturgical cycle.

NOTE

In BHS, the symbols for *sēḏer* and *pārāšāh* are always on the inside margin (toward the middle of the bound book.) Thus, on odd numbered pages, they will be found on the right side of the page, but will be on the left side of even numbered pages.

2
SPECIAL POINTS, UNUSUAL LETTERS, AND OTHER MARKS

PUNCTA EXTRAORDINARIA (special points)

The following passages contain special points found over words or letters. These probably indicate that doctrinal or textual reservations were held by the scribes. See Ginsberg, pp. 318–334 and Yeivin, articles 79–80 for more details.

Gen	16:5, 18:9, 19:33, 33:4, 37:12	Isa 44:9
Num	3:39, 9:10, 21:30, 29:15	Ezek 41:20, 46:22
Deut	29:28	Ps 27:13
2 Sam	19:20	

UNUSUAL LETTERS

Inverted Nûn

Num 10:34 and 10:36 are followed by an upside down *nûn* with a dot over it. Scholars believe that this sign was used to express doubt as to the correct sequence of the text. The sign also occurs seven times in Psalms 107, before verses 21, 22, 23, 24, 25, 26, and 40. It does not occur elsewhere in the Hebrew Bible.

Large Letters

Different manuscripts would occasionally use enlarged letters for a variety of purposes. Only a few of these have been reproduced in BHS. It was common, for example, for the first word of a book or section to be enlarged, although this is not done in BHS. The large letters may draw attention to statistical points, such as the large *wāw* in Lev 11:42, which marks the mid-point of the Torah in letters. The large *ʿayin* and *dālet̠* in Deut 6:4 probably call attention to an important passage or warn that the reading must be precise. In a case such as this, one would expect that the first and last words of the passage would be the ones to be enlarged. It has been suggested by some that since this would have resulted in the enlargement of a *šîn* and a *dālet̠* and would bring to mind the word שֵׁד meaning "demon," that it was decided to enlarge the last letter of the first word instead. This brings to mind the word עֵד meaning "witness" or "testimony." In other cases, such as the large final *nûn* in Num 27:5, the reason for the large letters is lost to antiquity. See Mynatt, p. 213 regarding Deut 32:4.

Small Letters

Small letters were used less commonly, apparently for purposes similar to the large letters. BHS contains only three, all final *nûn*'s, in Isa 44:14, Jer 39:13, and Prov 16:28.

Raised Letters

Four letters in the Bible are written above the normal line. They are the nûn in Judg 18:30, and *ʿayin*'s in Ps 80:14 and Job 38:13 and 15. According to Yeivin, the *nûn* of Manasseh (Judg 18:30) was most likely intended by the scribes to change משה (Moses) to מנשה in order to avoid mentioning Moses in connection with descendants of his who became idol priests. The *ʿayin* of Ps 80:14 may have been raised to mark it as the middle letter of the book of

Psalms. There is no obvious reason for the two other raised letters. See Yeivin, article 83.

OTHER MARKS

Pasēq [|]

The *pasēq* (or *pasîq*) is a vertical stroke that separates two words. Although not properly an accent, it is related to the accentual system in that it signifies that a pause should be made in the reading (*pasēq* means "divider") and that it may affect the accentuation and/or the pointing of the second word. In addition, *pasēq* may interact with certain accent marks so that the two in combination are treated as a distinct accent (see p. 30, 33-34, *lᵉḡarmeh*, et al). Note that Gesenius was careful to distinguish the "stroke" that follows composite accents from *pasēq* proper. However, BHS and most modern scholars commonly refer to this mark as *pasēq* wherever it is found. According to Gesenius, *pasēq* proper (i.e., when it is not part of an accent) is often used in the following situations (but may also be otherwise used):

1. An identical letter occurs at the end of the preceding word and the beginning of the following word.
2. The two words are identical or very similar.
3. The two words are absolutely contradictory.
4. The two words are liable to be wrongly connected.
5. The two words are heterogeneous terms (i.e., Eleazor, the high priest).

See Gesenius footnote 2 to section 15f and Yeivin articles 283–285 for more details about pasēq.

Maqqēp̄ [־]

Like *pasēq*, the *maqqēp̄* is not properly an accent, but is related to the accentual system in that it binds two words together into a single accentual unit. (*Maqqēp̄* means "joiner.") It most commonly follows short monosyllabic prepositions and conjunctions, but may also be used in other contexts. Beginning students often tend to view *maqqēp̄* as the mark of a noun in the construct state. However, construct nouns may be followed by *maqqēp̄* or they may have conjunctive accents instead. Moreover, since *maqqēp̄* is used in other situations, it is not possible to reliably deduce syntactical or other grammatical forms solely on the basis of its presence or absence. See Gesenius section 16 or Yeivin articles 290–306 for more details.

Metheg [ֽ]

The metheg (also called *gaʿyāʾ* or *maʾarîḵ*) is a short vertical stroke under the word. In BHK, it was placed to the left of the vowel to indicate that it appeared in Codex Leningradensis, and to the right of the vowel to indicate that it was supplied by the editors of BHK. This practice was discontinued in BHS and the metheg is simply put to the right or left of the vowel as it appears in Codex Leningradensis without supplementation by the editors. There appears to be no significant difference between *metheg* to right or left of the vowel. Most often, the *metheg* indicates a secondary stress in the word, but may also be used to indicate that the vowel should be fully pronounced and the pronunciation of the syllable should be slowed down. (The word *maʾarîḵ* means "lengthener," *gaʿyāʾ* means "raising" of the voice, and *metheg* means "bridle.") *Metheg* is a helpful clue to identifying two ambiguous vowel forms. The presence of metheg distinguishes *qāmeṣ* from *qāmeṣ ḥāṭûp̄* (since the latter can not occur in a stressed syllable). [However, note a few exceptions in Gesenius section 9v.] Similarly, the presence of *metheg* is an indication that what appears to be a simple *hîreq* is actually a defectively written naturally long *hîreq* (Gesenius sections 9g and 16i). See Gesenius section 16 and Yeivin articles 311–357 for a more detailed discussion of *metheg*.

> **NOTE**
>
> Do not confuse *metheg* with *sillûq*. *Sillûq* is similar in appearance, but always appears on the last accented syllable of a verse. See pp. 27, 31 regarding *sillûq*.

Rāp̄eh [̄]

The *rāp̄eh* is a horizontal line over a letter. It is not an accent. It is the opposite of *dagesh* (*lene* or *forte*) and *mappîq*. (*Rāp̄eh* means "softener.") In some manuscripts, every BGDKPT letter had either a *dagesh* or a *rāp̄eh*. Non-consonantal ה and א also had *rāp̄eh*, and it was used in a few other circumstances as well. Some of these situations can result in a BGDKPT letter having both a dagesh and a *rāp̄eh* (e.g., Deut 5:17 תּֿרצח). You will find *rāp̄eh* mentioned in the Mp; however, it has been almost entirely eliminated from BHS, even though it is common in Codex Leningradensis. An example of *rāp̄eh* occurring in the printed text may be found in 2 Sam 11:1 המּלאֿכים. See Yeivin, articles 397–399 for more details.

3
MASORA

THE MASORETES

Sometime around 500 CE (scholars cite dates ranging from 300 to 700), as the body of rabbinic teaching was being codified and the Mishnah produced, a new type of Hebrew biblical scholar began to assume the responsibility for preserving and transmitting the biblical text. In this role, these scholars supplanted the scribes, who had traditionally traced their history back to the work of Ezra. The new scholars incorporated vowel points and accent marks on their manuscripts. They also developed a system of notations in the margins of the text that provided both exegetical and text critical information. These notations were called the *massorah* (henceforth referred to in this guide with the Latin spelling "masora.") Some scholars have traced the word *massorah* to the root אסר, which means "to bind" and which suggests that the masora is a sort of fence that protects the scripture. Others trace the word to the root מסר, which means "to hand down." In this view, the term means "tradition." In either case, these scholars were remarkable for the techniques that they perfected over time to prevent corruption of the text, for their phenomenal knowledge of what modern students might consider textual "trivia," for their devotion to the preservation of the consonantal biblical text and for their conservative approach to its study.

The term *sopherim* ("those who count"), which had been the title of the scribes, came to be applied to those who wrote the consonantal text. Those who provided the vowel points and accents were called *nakdanim* ("pointers"). Those who provided the masora were called the masoretes. For a given manuscript, these three functions might be performed by three different people. Or two people might collaborate, with one of them performing two functions. In some cases, a single individual labored at all three tasks. Modern scholars often refer to all three functions under the general title "masorete."

The work of the masoretes extended over a period of about five hundred years. It included comparison of manuscripts and debates that had the effect of progressively eliminating variations in the pointing of the text and of agreeing upon the solutions to difficulties with the consonantal text that had been inherited from the scribes. By the end of the masoretic period, there was a virtual textus receptus agreed upon within the Western tradition. Initially there were at least two textual traditions divided along East/West lines. The Eastern tradition was associated with Babylon and at different times had centers at Nehardea, Sura, and Pumbedita. The Western tradition was associated with Palestine. Its most important center was at Tiberias. It is thus often called the Tiberian tradition and its masoretes are referred to as the Tiberian masoretes. (Some scholars hold that the Tiberian tradition was sufficiently distinct to be called a separate tradition. Therefore, they refer to three schools, the Babylonian, the Palestinian and the Tiberian.) Over the course of these centuries, the West became the spiritual leader of Judaism. By the time of the Middle Ages, the Eastern tradition was all but forgotten and remained so for nearly a thousand years until scholarly study of the Babylonian tradition was revived.

One of the most important families of the Tiberian masoretes was the Ben Asher family. It was once thought that the work of another important Tiberian masorete, Ben Naphtali, represented an opposing school to that of the Ben Ashers, but recently scholars have agreed that the two were closely related. One of the most respected texts of the era was that of Moses ben Asher. Reportedly, it contained only a few minor differences from a subsequent Ben Naphtali manuscript. The last major work of the Tiberian masoretes was that of Aaron ben Asher (son of Moses ben Asher). It was one of his manuscripts that was claimed to be the exemplar for the manuscript that is reproduced in BHS (see pp. 18–19).

Many students reading the Hebrew Bible do not pay much attention to the masora. Indeed, a brief glance at the marginal notes reveals it to be largely a collection of rather esoteric counts of words, combinations, and forms. In an age of printed texts in which we must struggle to even imagine the difficulties facing those who continually fought against the accidental intrusion of errors into the text, such information does not often draw our interest. However, the student who reads the masora will also find much in it that is of interest and is exegetically significant. If one is careful not to accept the masoretic comments any less critically than we would those of a modern editor, there is no reason why we should not benefit from the centuries of masoretic scholarship. This guide was therefore written with the hope that students will be encouraged to read more of the masora.

MASORA FINALIS

Most scholars reserve the term "masora finalis" to refer exclusively to the alphabetical lists taken from the Mm that appeared at the end of the Ben Chayim Rabbinic Bible (see p. 18). This arrangement was an innovation by Ben Chayim and does not appear in the manuscripts. However, you will occasionally find the term also applied to masoretic lists that follow each book of the Hebrew Bible. (Note that BHS numbers Samuel, Kings, Chronicles, and Ezra-Nehemiah as two books each in accordance with Christian Old Testament book and chapter divisions. In the Hebrew Bible, however, these are each one book. Thus there are no lists after 1 Samuel, 1 Kings, Ezra, or 1 Chronicles.) These lists are usually merely a count of the verses of the book, but they may also include additional information about the book or about larger sections of the text. For instance, following Deuteronomy is a note stating that the book has 955 verses, that its midpoint occurs at עַל־פִּי in verse 17:10, that it has 31 *sᵉdārîm* and that in the Torah as a whole there are 5,845 verses, 167 *sᵉdārîm,* 79,856 words and 400,945 letters. These entries were a form of quality control for the scribes who could check to ensure that a new manuscript conformed to the counts. The entries in BHS often have supplementary information that is not found in Codex Leningradensis, but is found in other manuscripts.

MASORA MARGINALIS

These were notes that the masoretes put in the margins around the text. The masora in the side margins have come to be called the masora parva (the small masora), abbreviated Mp. The masora at the top and bottom of the page came to be called the masora magna (the large masora), abbreviated Mm. The notes contained comments about the text, preserved non-textual traditions, identified infrequently appearing words or combinations, identified the midpoint of books or larger sections, pointed out other statistical information and contained concordance-like lists.

Masora Parva (Mp)

These are found in the outside margins of BHS (i.e., on the right edge of even numbered pages and the left edge of odd numbered pages). They are mostly written in Aramaic (with some Hebrew) and have been considerably supplemented beyond those found in Codex Leningradensis, which is the manuscript whose text is reproduced in BHS (see pp. 18–19). For the beginning or intermediate student, their most immediately useful purpose is to point out *qᵉrê* (see p. 13).

Associating Mp notes to the text. The small circles above the words in the text identify the portion of the text that is addressed by the Mp alongside that line. A single circle above a word near its center indicates that one or more notes in the margin refer to that word. If there is more than one word on the line with a circle above it, periods are used to separate the marginal notes for the different words. If the note applies to a phrase rather than a single word, there will be a circle spaced between each consecutive word in the phrase, but there will be only the one marginal note. If you discover two circles between adjacent words, it means that there is an additional note that refers to part of that phrase. The first note refers to the entire phrase and the second note refers to the sub-phrase, which starts at the double circles and usually (but not always) extends to the end of the larger phrase. This ambiguity about where the sub-phrase terminates occasionally makes it difficult to determine which notes relate to which words. The small raised numbers following the Mp notes do not refer to chapters or verses, but are related to the Mm (see the discussion of Mm on pp. 16–17).

> NOTE
>
> Do not confuse the Mp circles with the two accents, *tᵉlîšāʾ gᵉḏôlāh* and *tᵉlîšāʾ qᵉṭannāh* (see pp. 31-32).

Qᵉrê* and *Kᵉṯîḇ. In instances where the consonantal text was felt to be unsatisfactory or where textual variants were deemed to be worthy of preservation, the masoretes (who were bound not to alter the consonantal text) provided the consonants of the word to be read in the margin. The vowel points for the word to be read were then placed under the consonants written in the text. This can result in strange looking words if you don't remember that the vowel points under the ketîb belong to another word. The traditional consonantal form is called the *kᵉṯîḇ* (*kᵉṯîḇ* = "written") and the form in the margin is called the *qᵉrê* (*qᵉrê* = "to be read"). Because the masoretes intended that the *qᵉrê* form be automatically read without hesitation, the Mp for *qᵉrê* is a distinctive two-tiered arrangement that enhances recognition. A *qop̄* with a dot above it (קׄ, which is the abbreviation for *qᵉrê*) will be below the word(s) to be read in the margin. (See Gen 8:17 for an example.) There are hundreds of *qᵉrê* in the Hebrew Bible, and there are many different reasons for them. They may be euphemisms for indelicate or obscene words, they may provide the regular form for unusual or defectively written ones, they may protect the divine name or preclude readings that were felt to be inconsistent with respect to God, and they may provide "modern" corrections to archaic spellings. Don't forget that the vowel points in the text are for the *qᵉrê*, not the *kᵉṯîḇ*. The vowels belonging to the words of the *kᵉṯîḇ* are nowhere indicated by the masoretes, but are sometimes given by the editor in the critical apparatus at the bottom of the page.

Perpetual *Qᵉrê*. There are a few words that were intended to be read differently than the consonantal text throughout the Hebrew Bible or portions of it. Individual *qᵉrê* notes in the Mp are not provided for each occurrence of these words, but the vowel points are provided in the text.

K	

K^e^ṯîḇ (with *qerê* vowels)	Perpetual *q^e^rê*
יְהוָה	אֲדֹנָי
יְהוִה	אֱלֹהִים
הִוא	הִיא
יְרוּשָׁלַםִ	יְרוּשָׁלַיִם
יִשָּׂשכָר	יִשָּׂכָר
* (הַ)נַּעֲרָ	* (הַ)נַּעֲרָה

*Deuteronomy has Mp *q^e^rê* notes, see Mynatt, pp. 62-64, also pp. 139-140.

Unique Words and Phrases. Forms of words that occur only once in the Hebrew Bible are noted in Mp by ל̇, which is the abbreviation for לית, itself a contraction of לא אית meaning "there is no (other)." The same symbol is used to note groups of words that occur only once. In this case, the circles in the text will be between all the relevant words. Words or phrases occurring twice are noted by ב̇, which is the numeral 2; those occurring three times by ג̇, etc.

Hebrew Numbers. A dot above a Hebrew letter in Mp indicates that the letter is either an abbreviation or a numeral. The two most common abbreviations are ק̇ = *q^e^rê* and ל̇ = no other. The *q^e^rê* can easily be distinguished from a numeral by its two-tier arrangement. If there is no word above the ק̇, it's a numeral. ל̇ by itself always indicates a unique occurrence. It is never a numeral, except in combination.

Numbers may be read using the chart on the back cover of this guide. Simply add together the value of the numerals within an expression. For instance, מ̇ה̇ = 45 and ת̇פ̇ז̇ = 487. Numbers are normally formed by placing the higher value numerals to the right of lesser values. An exception is 15, which is written ה̇י̇ rather than י̇ה̇. This was done in order to avoid resemblance to the divine name. To avoid confusion with the sign of a unique occurrence, the number 30 is written כ̇י̇, not ל̇.

Translating Mp. The Words in Mp can be translated by referring to the index in BHS pages L-LV. Unfortunately for most American students, the index translates into Latin. Therefore, English translations have been provided in chapter 6 of this guide. Abbreviations in Mp are indicated by dots above a letter or by double strokes (״). Thus פּֽתׄ = פתח = *pataḥ* and ד״ה = דברי הימים = the book of Chronicles.

Seberin. In several cases, the Mp note סביׄר ("supposed" or "expected") precedes a correction in the margin of an unusual form found in the text. An example can be found in Gen 19:23. Some scholars believe that the *seberin* indicate corrections that have been proposed, but which the masoretes considered to be incorrect. In this case, the text, not the Mp, would contain the "approved" reading of the masoretes. See Yeivin, article 109, and Roberts, p. 36 for two different views of *seberin*.

Tiqqune Sopherim. The masoretes believed that early in the textual history some changes were made in the text in order to avoid disrespect to the deity, and attributed eighteen such changes to the early scribes. They called these *tiqqune sopherim* (scribal corrections). These may be noted in the Mp with the supposed original supplied in the margin. The words *tiqqune sopherim* may or may not appear in BHS Mp. *Tiqqune sopherim* (abbreviated Tiq Soph) may also be identified in the BHS critical apparatus.

***Itture Sopherim* (scribal omissions)**. There are a few places in the Bible in which the conjunction *wāw* is expected, but does not appear. These instances are known by scholars as *itture sopherim*. In BHS, they are not identified as such, but the *wāw* is suggested by the critical apparatus (see pp 19–20). An example is אַחַר in Gen 18:5. In addition, there are a few passages in which the masoretes supplied words that they believed the scribes had omitted from the text. These are identified in BHS with the Mp note "קׄ ולא כתׄ" meaning "to be read though not written." An example can be found in 2 Sam 16:23. The traditional view regarding the missing *wāw*'s is that the scribes removed the conjunction in those places at which they believed it had been erroneously used. However, a great deal of ambiguity surrounds the *itture sopherim*. There are many places in the Bible in which the conjunction *wāw* might have been unnecessarily added to a word, and a great many in which various manuscripts differ in using or not using *wāw*. Scholars do not agree on why these few cases were uniquely designated. There is uncertainty as to what should be considered the number of *itture sopherim* and there are differences of opinion regarding the precise difference between *itture sopherim* and the *qᵉrê*/*kᵉṯîḇ* system. For different views of *itture sopherim*, see Würthwein, p. 19; Ginsberg, pp. 308–9; and Yeivin article 91.

Masora Magna (Mm)

The masora magna are not included in the same volume as the BHS text, but are published in a separate volume titled *Massorah Gedolah*. It consists mostly of lists of words, somewhat resembling a concordance. Beginning or intermediate students will rarely find it useful. Entry to the Mm from the text is through the Mp. A circle over a word directs you to the Mp. At the end of the Mp note, if there is a small raised numeral, it directs you to the appropriate note below the page of text (but above the BHS critical apparatus, which is at the very bottom of the page). This note usually directs you to a particular list in *Massorah Gedolah*. As an example, on the first page of the text of BHS, in Gen 1:5, there is a small "12" after the first Mp note for that line. Looking below the text, we are referred to Mm list number 3105, which can be found in *Massorah Gedolah*, and which lists the seven places in the Hebrew Bible in which the word לָאוֹר occurs. There are other types of relationships between Mp and Mm than this simple example. These are fully discussed in Mynatt, chapter 1. If you desire to use *Massorah*

Gedolah, also read BHS pp. XV-XVII, which contain a thorough description of the relationship between the BHS text and *Massorah Gedolah*. Note, however, that although the discussion in BHS refers to three volumes of *Massorah Gedolah*, only the first volume was ever published. Therefore, if the note in the Mp is not indexed to one of the lists in vol. 1 of *Massorah Gedolah*, you will find the note *sub loco* at the bottom of the page above the critical apparatus. This simply means that a masoretic note occurs at that place. It was supposed to be discussed in the never published third volume of *Massorah Gedolah*. According to the editor of the BHS masora, these notes pose "no special problems of form or content." Every one of the sub loco notes in the Torah has been analyzed and discussed by Mynatt in *The Sub Loco Notes in the Torah of Biblia Hebraica Stuttgartensia*.

4
BHS CRITICAL APPARATUS

RELATIONSHIP OF THE TEXT TO MANUSCRIPTS

The second Rabbinic Bible was published in Venice in 1524/25, only eight years after its predecessor. It was apparently based upon twelfth century or later manuscripts and was edited by Jacob ben Chayim. From the time of its publication until 1936, it was the virtual *textus receptus* for both Jews and Christians. [A Rabbinic Bible contains the Masoretic Text (with masora), the Targums, and rabbinic commentaries all on the same page.] The first two editions of BHK were based upon the Ben Chayim text; but with the publication of the third edition in 1936, a different source was used. Like the third edition of BHK, the BHS text is a reproduction of Codex Leningradensis, a medieval manuscript in the Tiberian tradition dating to about 1008 CE. One man, Samuel ben Jacob, is claimed by its colophon to have written, pointed and provided the masora for the manuscript. (A colophon is a short statement at the end of a manuscript that provides details about the masoretes, the sources used, the date of its completion, or other information about the manuscript. A codex is a manuscript with separate pages in book form as opposed to a scroll. While scrolls can still be found in synagogues, the codices began to replace the scrolls for popular use around the seventh or eighth century CE.) The colophon of Codex Leningradensis also claims that the manuscript represents the Ben Asher tradition, a claim justified by recent research. The significance of Codex Leningradensis is that it is the oldest known manuscript of the complete Hebrew Bible based upon the Ben Asher tradition. Codex Leningradensis is provided in BHS without significant alteration. The critical apparatus at the bottom of the pages in BHS indicates portions where other manuscripts or versions differ or where scholarly research brings the BHS text into question. The critical apparatus for different books of the Bible were compiled by different editors. The editor of each book is identified on the back of the title page of BHS.

ASSOCIATING ENTRIES TO THE TEXT

The critical apparatus is keyed to small raised letters of the English alphabet that appear within the text. A small letter immediately following a word indicates that the associated critical note applies to the preceding word only. A small letter may also appear under a *maqqēp̄*, in which case the note applies to the word up to the *maqqēp̄*. If the small letter immediately precedes a word, one of two situations is indicated. If the word is the first word of a verse and the small letter is not repeated in that verse, then the critical note applies to the entire verse. If the small letter is repeated, regardless of whether or not the word is the first word of the verse, then the critical note applies to all the text between the first and second instances of the same small letter.

The small letters start anew in sequence with "a" for each new verse (unless a note carries over to the following verse). Thus there will be several a's, b's, c's, etc. on a single page. It is therefore necessary to ensure that the small letter in the apparatus follows the correct verse (indicated by boldface numbers in the apparatus) and the correct chapter (indicated by a boldface "Cp" and the chapter number in the apparatus). Each individual note is separated from the subsequent note by a set of parallel vertical lines (||).

TRANSLATING THE SYMBOLS

Most of the symbols used in the critical apparatus are explained in BHS, pp. XLIV-L. The more common of these are also included at the end of Rüger's *An English Key*. When citing sources, the apparatus will use a symbol that indicates a major tradition (called "versions," such as Septuagint, Samaritan Pentateuch, etc.). This may or may not be followed by superscript symbols that identify specific manuscripts. (If no version or manuscript is referred to, the note following is a suggestion by the editor of the critical apparatus for that book.) Unfortunately, not all the symbols used are explained in BHS and the same symbols may sometimes be used in different ways by different editors. Wonneberger's *Understanding BHS* can be consulted for a complete explanation of all symbols appearing in BHS. An efficient method of entering Wonneberger's work for this purpose is to turn first to the index of symbols on pp. 87–88.

The following is a list of a few of the more common symbols used but not explained in BHS that will usually suffice for the beginning student.

- a minus sign in the superscript of a source citation indicates that the note applies to the tradition cited *except for* those manuscripts listed after the minus sign.

? a question mark may indicate that the entry is a question or that the statement contained in the entry is uncertain. Note: the Latin "num" may also be used to indicate that the entry is a question.

= the equal sign is used to explain or to offer conjecture about the derivation of a form or translation.

|| parallel vertical lines are used to separate entries.

, ; commas or semicolons are used to separate the parts of an entry. (There is no apparent difference between comma and semicolon.)

/ the slash may indicate that the entry refers to two verses (whose numbers will be on either side of the slash), or it may indicate that the following is an abbreviated presentation of differing forms, or it may simply separate items in respective relationship.

° a superscript circle indicates that the preceding number is an ordinal (first, second, etc.) rather than a verse citation.

( ) parentheses are used to enclose:
— citations relating to the edition quoted, or
— abbreviated presentations of differing forms, or
— explanatory notes, or
— symbols for versions that bear the general, but not literal, meaning of the following note.

NOTE

The symbols Ms and Mss always refer to *Hebrew* manuscripts.

VALUE JUDGMENTS IN TEXT CRITICISM

In most cases, the BHS editors simply provide variant readings without an evaluation of the relative worth of the version or manuscript in which they appear. Of course, such a decision can be the work of a lifetime and may be subject to considerable controversy. Textual criticism involves the careful consideration of numerous issues that are beyond the scope of this guide. It never reduces to an uncritical acceptance of one reading over another simply because of the version in which it appears. Nevertheless, beginning students may benefit from the following list which, according to Würthwein, p.112, indicates in descending value "roughly the order of their significance for textual criticism."

Masoretic Text
Samaritan Pentateuch
Septuagint
Aquila
Symmachus
Theodotion
Syriac
Targums
Vulgate
Old Latin
Sahidic
Coptic
Ethiopic
Arabic
Armenian

TRANSLATING ABBREVIATIONS AND LATIN

Rüger's *An English Key* is invaluable. If you do not have a command of Latin, you should have a copy of it beside you whenever you read BHS. For this reason, it has been included as an appendix to this guide. Simply look up the Latin words or abbreviations in the key to obtain the English translation. When looking up abbreviations, remember that they may or may not be listed in the proper alphabetical order of the entire word that they represent. For instance, the letter "c" is the abbreviation for "cum" (meaning "with"). It will be found not at the beginning of the c's, but near the end. The remaining portion of abbreviated words are shown in parenthesis.

The following is a list of a few words or abbreviations that are either not included in Rüger's key or that require further explanation. Wonneberger's *Understanding BHS* can be consulted for a complete discussion of the BHS critical apparatus.

1. *ast(eriscus) and ob(elus)* are included in Rüger's key but are simply translated as "asterisk" and "obelus" respectively. Beginning students may wish to know that the asterisk and obelus were symbols used in Origen's Hexapla. The asterisk was the initial bracket for corrective additions from the Hebrew. The obelus was the initial bracket for corrective deletions when the Septuagint contained material lacking in the Hebrew. There was an additional symbol (called metobelus) to close the bracket for both asterisk and obelus, but it is not referred to in BHS. The Hexapla was the Old Testament in six parallel columns. The first column contained the Hebrew text. The second contained a transliteration of the Hebrew into Greek. The other columns contained the Greek Septuagint and three revisions of it. The work was enormous (more than 6,000 pages) and probably was rarely, if ever, copied in its entirety. No authentic manuscript of the Hexaplaric Septuagint has survived. Nevertheless, the Hexapla is a major consideration in biblical criticism because of the numerous copies of column five, the Septuagint, that were made and because of the extensive reliance on them by early and medieval Christians. Because the asteriscus, obelus, and metobelus were meaningless without the other columns, they were frequently omitted over time until eventually most manu-

scripts omitted them entirely. Using such manuscripts, it was not possible to determine which passages reflected the Hebrew text and which reflected the Septuagint. Today the term "hexaplaric" is used pejoratively by biblical scholars.

2. *fut* = future

3. *hi* = *hiphil*

4. *hit* = *hithpael*

5. *ho* = *hophal*

6. *K* = *k*ᵉ*ṯîḇ*

7. *ni* = *niphal*

8. *num* = indicates that the entry is a question

9. *ob* = (see "ast" - #1)

10. *pi* = *piel*

11. *pu* = *pual*

12. Q = *q*ᵉ*rê*

13. *Seb* = *s*ᵉ*bîr* (see p. 15)

14. *Tiq Soph* = (*tiqqune sopherim*) means "scribal corrections" (see p. 15)

5
THE ACCENTS

GENERAL

There are two accentual systems in the Hebrew Bible. Psalms, Proverbs, and most of Job constitute the "Three Books" of poetry. These books have their own system of accents, which differs somewhat from that of the remaining "Twenty-One Books." Accents serve three purposes. Primarily they are musical (or cantillation) marks, but they also indicate accentuation and semantic division. Pages 35–36 below discuss the musical values of the accents. This and the following two paragraphs discuss accentuation and semantic division. Although not properly accent marks, *pasēq*, *maqqēp̄* and *metheg* are related to the accent system in differing ways. These marks are discussed on pages 5–6.

The accents are divided into two groups called "disjunctive" and "conjunctive." The disjunctive accents are usually on the last word of a phrase, clause, or other semantic unit. Note that semantic units (i.e., units of meaning) do not always coincide with syntactical units. Thus an *'aṯnaḥ*, for example, may occur in the middle of a clause, but usually signifies some discrete sense of meaning. (The word "unit" in the tables on the following pages refers to semantic units as distinguished from purely syntactical.) In general terms, the accents listed under "group 1" on the following pages divide the verse; the accents under "group 2" divide the two halves; the accents in "group 3" are subordinate to those in "group 2"; etc. As a general rule, only those accents in "group 1" and perhaps those in "group 2" should be taken into consideration in translation at the beginning or intermediate level. One should usually translate all the words up to one of these major disjunctive accents and form them into a unit of meaning before proceeding on to subsequent words.

The conjunctive accents are used on the words between the disjunctive accents and do not divide semantic units. Conjunctive accents indicate some sort of connection to the next word. The conjunctive accents are often referred to as servi (servants) for the disjunctive accents. Some disjunctive accents may take only a limited or specific number of servi. Servi precede the disjunctive accent that they "serve." Note that in the following tables, the number of permissible servi are usually indicated for each disjunctive accent. Often, the type of servi that may be used are also indicated. In these cases, there is no relationship between the number of servi that may be used and the number of types of servi that may be used. For instance, *tᵉḇîr* may have up to four servi, but this does not mean that each one of the four conjunctives listed must be used with each occurrence of *tᵉḇîr*. The conjunctives listed may be used in different combinations and permutations.

The accent marks found in BHS are somewhat stylized. They resemble but are not always identical in shape to those marks found in the manuscripts. The position of the accents, however, follows the manuscripts. Every word has some sort of accent sign (or *maqqēp̄*) and may have more than one. [Note that two traditions of accentuation are preserved in Gen 35:22 and the Decalogue (in Exodus 20 and Deuteronomy 5). Thus, you will find words there that have two conjunctive or two disjunctive accents.] Most accents (either disjunctive or conjunctive) are placed under or over the syllable that receives the primary stress. Usually an accent below the word appears to the left of the vowel if the accented letter has a vowel. A few accents (marked below as "prepositive") appear on the first letter of the word or (marked "postpositive") on the last letter. In these cases, the syllable to receive the primary stress must be determined independently of the accent mark.

THE ACCENTS OF THE TWENTY-ONE BOOKS

The following tables summarize in very general terms the semantic use of accents in the Twenty-One Books. The rules governing which servi may precede a disjunctive and in what sequence are sometimes rather complex. Therefore, this guide for the most part simply lists the names of conjunctive accents. These tables are provided as a matter of convenience for those students who may be interested. Most students will find little value in attempting to remember the names of all the accents, although they may benefit from perusal of these pages. For more detailed information on accents, read Wickes, Yeivin articles 176–357, and Gesenius section 15.

Disjunctive Accents of the Twenty-One Books

Group 1:

XXX (stroke below)	*sillûq*	Identifies the last accented syllable of a verse. Only one servus (*mêrᵉḵāʾ*).
XXX (^ below)	*ʾaṯnaḥ*	(or *atnach* or *etnach*). Divides verse. May be replaced by *zāqēp̄* or *ṭip̄ḥāh* for short verses. Usually only one servus (*mûnaḥ*).

> **NOTE**
>
> *ʾaṯnaḥ* and *sillûq* sometimes call for changes in the way a word is pointed in order to reflect a slowing of the reading (or a pause). These are called pausal forms. To further confuse matters, pausal forms may also occasionally occur with *zāqēp̄* and *sᵉḡôltāʾ* or (rarely) even with other disjunctive accents. An example of a *zāqēp̄* pausal form may be found in Judg 1:15 (נְתַתָּנִי for נְתַתַּנִי).

Group 2:

XXX	*ṭip̄ḥāh*	Divides units between *ʾaṯnaḥ* and *sillûq*, when main division comes on first word preceding *ʾaṯnaḥ* or *sillûq*. If *zāqēp̄* divides the unit, *ṭip̄ḥāh* divides units between *zāqēp̄* and *ʾaṯnaḥ* or *sillûq*. One servus (*mêrᵉḵāʾ*) or none.
XXX	*zāqēp̄ qāṭōn* (or *qāṭan*)	Divides two units formed by *ʿaṯnaḥ*, when the division precedes *ʾaṯnaḥ* or *sillûq* by more than one word. Usually has one or two servi (*mûnaḥ*). Most common accent of 21 books.

XXX	*zāqēp̄ gāḏôl*	Has same semantic value as *zāqēp̄ qāṭōn* but different musical value.
XXX	*sᵉḡôltāʾ* (POSTPOSITIVE)	May be first major division in the first half of verse (i.e., replaces first *zāqēp̄*). May be followed by but not preceded by *zāqēp̄*. Is always preceded by *zarqāʾ*. One or two servi (*mûnaḥ*).
XXX	*šalšeleṯ*	Replaces *sᵉḡôltāʾ* when *sᵉḡôltāʾ* would appear on first word of verse. (Used only seven times in the 21 books.)

Group 3:

XXX	*rᵉḇîᵃʿ*	*Divides zāqēp̄, sᵉḡôltāʾ* or *ṭip̄ḥāh* units. Can be repeated to indicate further division. Up to 3 servi (*mûnaḥ, dargāʾ*).
XXX	*zarqāʾ* (POSTPOSITIVE)	Precedes *sᵉḡôltāʾ*. May be major division of *sᵉḡôltāʾ* unit or, if *rᵉḇîᵃʿ is major division, comes between rᵉḇîᵃʿ and sᵉḡôltāʾ*. May come between 2 *rᵉḇîᵃʿ* in *sᵉḡôltāʾ* unit. May be repeated for further division. Up to 4 servi (*mûnaḥ, ʾazlāʾ*, *mêrᵉḵāʾ, tᵉlîšāʾ qᵉṭannāh*)

XXX (accent above)	*paštā*ʾ (POSTPOSITIVE)	May divide *zāqēp̄* unit. If *rᵉḇîaʿ* divides *zāqēp̄* unit, it comes between *rᵉḇîaʿ* and *zāqēp̄*. May also come between two *rᵉḇîaʿ*. Up to 6 servi (*mᵉhuppāḵ*, *mêrᵉḵāʾ*, *ʾazlāʾ*, *mûnaḥ*, *tᵉlîšāʾ qᵉṭannāh*). Postpositive position distinguishes it from *ʾazlāʾ*.
XXX (accent below)	*yᵉṯîḇ* (PREPOSITIVE)	Same semantic value as *paštāʾ* with different musical value. Prepositive position differentiates from *mᵉhuppāḵ*.
XXX (accent below)	*tᵉḇîr*	Divides units that end with *ṭip̄ḥāh*. If this unit is divided by *rᵉḇîaʿ*, it is on word preceding *ṭip̄ḥāh*. Up to 4 servi (*dargāʾ*, *mêrᵉḵāʾ*, *ʾazlāʾ*, *tᵉlîšāʾ qᵉṭannāh*).

Group 4:

XXX (accent above)	*gereš*	Subordinate to *rᵉḇîaʿ*, *paštāʾ*, *tᵉḇîr or zarqāʾ*. One or no servus (*mûnaḥ*).
XXX (accent above)	*gērᵉšayim*	Double *gereš*. Same semantic value as *gereš*, but different musical value.
|XXX	*lᵉḡarmeh*	Symbol is *mûnaḥ* combined with *paseq*. Usually divides unit that ends with *rᵉḇîaʿ*. 1 or 2 servi.

XXX	*pāzēr qāṭōn* (or *qāṭan*)	Subordinate to *r^{e}ḇî^{a}ʿ*, *pašṭāʾ*, *t^{e}ḇîr* or *zarqāʾ*. Up to 6 servi.
XXX	*pāzēr gāḏôl*	(Or *qarnê pārāh* = "cow-horns.") Subordinate to *r^{e}ḇî^{a}ʿ*, *pašṭāʾ*, *t^{e}ḇîr* or *zarqāʾ*. Up to 7 servi. Used only 16 times in Bible. See Ezra 6:9 for example.
XXX	*t^{e}lîšāʾ g^{e}ḏôlāh* (PREPOSITIVE)	Subordinate to *r^{e}ḇî^{a}ʿ*, *pašṭāʾ*, *t^{e}ḇîr* or *zarqāʾ*. Up to 5 servi.

Conjunctive Accents of the 21 Books

XXX	*mûnaḥ*
XXX	*m^{e}huppāḵ* (or *mehuppach* or *mahpak*)
XXX	*mêr^{e}ḵāʾ* (*merka*, *mercha*)
XXX	*dargāʾ*
XXX	*ʾazlāʾ*
XXX	*t^{e}lîšāʾ q^{e}ṭannāh* (POSTPOSITIVE)
XXX	*galgal* (or *yeraḥ*)
XXX	*mêr^{e}ḵāʾ ḵ^{e}pûlāh* (double *mêr^{e}ḵāʾ*)
XXX	*mâyᵉlāʾ* (or *m^{eʾ}ayy^{e}lāʾ*) Variant of *ṭip̄ḥāh*. Marks secondary accent in words with *sillûq* or *ʾaṯnaḥ*.

NOTE

Tᵉlîšā' gᵉḏôlāh is a small circle above the word with a tail below it slanting to the left. *Tᵉlîšā' qᵉṭannāh* is also a small circle above the word with its tail slanting to the right. Because the tails are so small, it is easy to confuse these accents with the circles that denote references to Mp. This confusion can be minimized by remembering that Mp references are near the center of a word or are equally spaced between two words. *Tᵉlîšā' qᵉṭannāh* immediately follows the last letter of a word and *tᵉlîšā' gᵉḏôlāh* immediately precedes the first letter.

THE ACCENTS OF THE THREE BOOKS

The "Three Books" are Psalms, Job, and Proverbs. The preceding discussion of accents in general applies to these three "poetic" books, but a different system of marking, with slightly different criteria, is employed. Some accent signs used in the Twenty-One Books are also used in the Three Books, but others are unique to the Three Books. The beginning and ending sections of Job (1:1 to 3:2 and 42:7–17) are considered to be prose and use the same system of accentuation as the Twenty-One Books. The following table summarizes in very general terms the semantic use of accents in the three books of poetry. For more details, see Wickes, and Yeivin articles 358–374.

Disjunctive Accents of the Three Books

XXX	*sillûq*	Used as in the Twenty-One Books, but up to 4 servi.
XXX	*ʿôleh w*^{e}*yôrēḏ*	Main verse division. Only 1 servus.
XXX	*ʾaṯnaḥ*	Divides 2nd half of verse or divides short verses. Up to 5 servi.
XXX	*r*^{e}*ḇî*^{a}*ʿ*	(*qāṭōn*) = used immediately before *ʿôleh w*^{e}*yôrēḏ*. (*gāḏôl*) = main divider of unit ending with *ʾaṯnaḥ*. *R*^{e}*ḇî*^{a}*ʿ* qāṭōn and *gāḏôl* have same symbol. May also be main verse divider for short verse with no *ʾaṯnaḥ*. Usually only one servus.
XXX	*r*^{e}*ḇî*^{a}*ʿ mug̱rāš*	Last disjunctive before *sillûq*.
|XXX	*šalšeleṯ g*^{e}*ḏôlāh*	Distinguished from *šalšeleṯ q*^{e}*ṭannāh* by *pasēq* following the word. Used in second half of verse preceding the two servi of *sillûq*. Usually has no servus.
XXX	*ṣinnôr* (POSTPOSITIVE)	(Also called *zarqāʾ*.) Divides *ʿôleh w*^{e}*yôrēḏ* unit. Up to two servi. Postpositive position distinguishes from *ṣinnôrîṯ*.

XXX ˎ	*dᵉḥî* (PREPOSITIVE)	Divides unit ending with *ʾatnaḥ*. Up to three servi. Prepositive position differentiates it from *ṭarḥāʾ*.
XXX	*pāzēr*	Subordinate to *rᵉbîᵃ͑ gādôl, dᵉḥî* and *ṣinnôr*. Up to 3 servi.
|XXX	*mᵉhuppāk lᵉḡarmeh*	Subordinate to *rᵉbîᵃ͑ gādôl, dᵉḥî* and *ṣinnôr*. Servi is *mᵉhuppāk*. Also used with no servus for short words. Looks like *mᵉhuppāk*, but *pasēq* follows word.
|XXX	*ʾazlāʾ lᵉḡarmeh*	Variant form of *lᵉḡarmeh*. Used with *ʾazlāʾ* servus or for long words with no servus. Looks like *ʾazlāʾ*, but has *pasēq*.

Conjunctive Accents of the Three Books

XXX	*mûnaḥ*
XXX	*mêrᵉkā* (*merka*)
XXX	*͑illûy* (also called *mûnaḥ* superior)
XXX	*ṭarḥāʾ*
XXX	*galgal* (*yeraḥ*)
XXX	*mᵉhuppāk*
XXX	*ʾazlāʾ*

XXX *šalšele*ṯ *q*^{e}*ṭannāh*

XXX *ṣinnôrî*ṯ (Not an independent accent. Used with *mêr*^{e}*ḵā*ʾ or *m*^{e}*huppāḵ*.)

CANTILLATION

A close relationship exists between the accent signs and the musical rendering of the Hebrew Bible. In general, each accent sign is associated with a group of notes, called "motives." However, the correspondence between a given sign and a particular motive is not a simple one. The rendering associated with an accent sign may vary considerably depending upon the book being cantillated, upon the content of the reading, upon the type of liturgical performance (wedding, pilgrimage festival, etc.), upon the medium of performance (individual cantillation, communal by congregation, etc.) and upon the regional tradition. In addition, a certain range of flexibility may be permitted for individual interpretation by the reader.

The *pasēq*, *maqqēp̄*, and *metheg* are not properly accents and have no musical motives of their own, but they establish certain relationships between the musical intonation and the text or between various accent related motives.

There are numerous musical traditions associated with the accent signs. The western ashkenazic, the sephardic (different in Egypt, France, Holland, etc.) the Persian, Syrian and others. These traditions may associate different motives to an accent as indicated by the following five examples for the ʾ*aṯnaḥ* in the Pentateuch.

Not only may motives differ between the two fundamental accentual systems (those of the Twenty-One Books and of the

Three Books), but the particular motive associated with an accent may also differ depending upon whether the text is the Pentateuch, the Prophets, one of the festal scrolls, etc.

Encyclopaedia Judaica has an excellent introductory article on this subject under the title "Masoretic Accents."

In addition to the traditional systems of cantillation, there have been many attempts through the years to recover musical information from the masoretic accentual system. The most recent such effort is that of Suzanne Haïk-Vantoura, a French musicologist and composer who has published several works and recordings. An English translation of the second edition of her book has been published under the title, *The Music of the Bible Revealed*. Haïk-Vantoura claims that each symbol has precise meaning in terms of musical expression and that the system as a whole predates the masoretes by several centuries.

6
INDEX OF SYMBOLS AND ABBREVIATIONS OF THE SMALL MASORA

(Translation based on BHS pp. L-LV)

Mp	TRANSLATION	OT REF
א״ב=אלפא ביתא	alphabet	
א ב ג......ת	Hebrew letters without points are consonants	
אׄ בׄ גׄ......תׄ	Hebrew letters with points are numbers	
אדכרה	mention of the divine name, tetragrammaton	Ps 119:115
אורׄ, אוריתׄ=אוריתא	Pentateuch	
אותׄ=אותיות	letters	
אותׄ תלויות	raised letters	Judg 18:30
אׄ זׄ ןׄ=אני, זאת, נא	Indicates that the word זכר occurs twice in Psalms other than those places where joined with one of these three words.	Ps 25:7
איוב	the book of Job	

איש רגלי	foot soldiers	Gen 30:30
אית	there is, there are	
אית בהון	there is in them, they contain	
אית בהון א״ב	all the letters of the alphabet are in them	
איתׄ=איתתא	wife, woman	
אכילה	noun from the verb אכל	Judg 7:24
אמירה	noun from the verb אמר	
אנש	man	
אריה	lion	Jer 39:7
ארמי	Aramaic	
את	sign of the accusative case	
אתנחׄ=אתנחתא	*ʾaṯnaḥ* (accent)	
ב	in, into	
בהון	in them	
באר	well, cistern	
ביאה	noun from the verb בוא	Jer 17:27
ביזה	plunder, booty	Isa 33:23
ביניהׄ=ביניהון	between them	
בכיה	noun from the verb בכה	2 Sam 1:24
בׄמׄ=בר מן	except	
בן אשר	Tiberian masoretic tradition descending from Ben Asher	Ps 31:12
בן נפתלי	Tiberian masoretic tradition descending from Ben Naphtali	Isa 44:20
בראשית	the book of Genesis	
ברנש	man	
בתר	after	
בתרׄ=בתרא	last	Num 35:15
געיא	*gaʿyāʾ* (*metheg*, secondary accent, see p. 6)	
גריש	*gereš* (accent)	

ד	Aramaic relative particle (as prefix = who, which, etc.)	
דגשׁ=דיגשא	dagesh	
דגשׁ א	*ʾalep̄* with dagesh (i.e., *mappîq*)	Gen 43:26
ד״ה=דברי הימים	the book of Chronicles	
דבור משה	every place in which וידבר יהוה אל משה or similar is written	Exod 16:34
דין	this	Lev 14:31
דל	poor, poor person	
דמיין	similar	Gen 41:26
ה̇י̇	the number 15 (not יה̇, never ט̇ו)	
הליכה	noun from the verb הלך	Gen 27:37
ו	and, and . . . also	
ויקרא	the book of Leviticus	
זה	this	
בזה	with this, in this	Job 5:27
זוגין	pairs (words or phrases united by some feature)	
זכר	masculine gender	
זעירין	small (of small letters)	
נונין זעירין	small letters nûn	Isa 44:14
ז̇ א̇ וס״פ=זקף אתנח̇ וסוף פסוק	*zāqēp̄*, *ʾat̠naḥ* and end of verse	
זקף פת̇	indicates syllable is accented by *zāqēp̄*, vowel *pat̠aḥ* is to be pronounced	
זקף קמ̇	indicates syllable is accented by *zāqēp̄*, vowel *qāmeṣ* is to be pronounced	

זרקא	*zarqāʾ*, *ṣinnôr* or *ṣinnôrîṯ*	
סמיכ̇ לזרקא	following *zarqāʾ* with *s^eḡôltāʾ*, see p. 29)	Gen 37:22
חד, חדה	one, once	
חד מן	one out of, one of	
חול	common, ordinary (not sacred)	Gen 26:4
חומש	Pentateuch	
חומש המגילות	the five *megilloth*, that is: Ruth, Song of Songs, Ecclesiastes, Lamentations, Esther	Lev 7:9
חטף	*ḥāṭēp̄*, half (i.e., short vowel, without metheg)	Jer 49:28
חלוף	discrepancy, variation; different form/order	Ruth 4:9
חס̇=חסר	defectively written	
וחס̇	and also defectively written	
חס̇ את	indicates that the sign of the accusative case is lacking	
חס̇ בן נבט	indicates name בן נבט is desired	1 Kgs 14:16
חס̇ דחס̇	word twice defectively written	Gen 45:22
חס̇ האלה	indicates word האלה is desired	Gen 24:66
חצי	half, middle	
חצי אותיות בתור̇	half the letters in the Pentateuch	Lev 11:42
חצי הנביאים	middle of the books of the prophets (by verses)	Isa 17:3
חצי הספר בפסוקים	middle of book by verses	

חצי התורה בפסוקׄ	middle of the Pentateuch by verses	Lev 8:8
חצי התורה בתיבות	middle of the Pentateuch by words	Lev 10:16
טנוף	soiled (with excrements, secretions, etc.)	Isa 30:22
טעׄ, טעמׄ=טעם, טעמין	accent	
בזה הטעׄ	with this accent	Job 5:27
בטעׄ דין	with this accent	Lev 14:31
בטעׄ לאחור	with prepositive accent	Lev 5:2
יהושע	the book of Joshua	
יחזקׄ=יחזקאל	the book of Ezekiel	
יי	tetragrammaton	
ירמיה	the book of Jeremiah	
ישעיה	the book of Isaiah	
יׄ שׄ תׄ=יהושע, שפטים, תלים	Joshua, Judges, Psalms	
יתיר	superfluous, paragogic (having a letter or syllable added to the last word). Literal meaning = "extra" or "more."	
יתיר ס״ת=יתיר סוף תיבותא	paragogic in the last	Josh 10:24
כותׄ=כותיה, כותיהון	like it, like them	
כׄ׳	the number 30 (not ל׳)	
כינוי ליצחק	cognomen of Isaac	Jer 33:26
כל	all, the whole	
כלייה	noun from the verb כלה	Deut 28:32
כן	so, thus	
כן כתׄ, כתׄ כן	thus written	

כל תורה כת֯ כן	thus written in all the Pentateuch	Gen 32:12
כפתוי דשמשון	the binding of Samson (indicates the pericope of the binding of Samson in Judg 15:12).	Gen 42:24
כת֯=כתיב	k^e*ṯîḇ* (written)	
כת֯ א, כת֯ ה	written letter **א**, written letter ה	
כתיב֯=כתיבין	The Writings (last of three major divisions of Hebrew Bible, also called Hagiographa)	
ל	sign of the dative case	
ל֯=לית	there is no (other), this word or combination of words does not occur except in this place. Has effective meaning of “once” or “unique.”	
דלית בהון	which are unique in it	Exod 20:13
לגר֯=לגרמיה	l^e*ḡarmeh* (accent)	
ליש֯,ליש֯נ=לישן, לישנין	language, meaning, similar forms	
תר֯י ליש֯נ=תרי לישנין	dual meaning	Exod 5:18
לפי מ֯ג֯=לפי מסורה גדולה	according to the large masora (Mm)	Zeph 1:1
לפי מ֯ק֯=לפי מסורה קטנה	according to the small masora (Mp)	Zeph 1:1
לשין	language, meaning, similar forms	
לשון אכילה	the meaning “to eat”	Judg 7:24

לשון אריה	the meaning "a lion"	Jer 39:7
לשון ארמי	in Aramaic language	
לשון ביאה	the meaning "to enter"	Jer 17:27
לשון ביזה	the meaning "plunder"	Isa 33:23
לשון בכיה	the meaning "weep"	2 Sam 1:24
לשון דל	the meaning "poverty"	
לשון הליכה	the meaning "anger"	Gen 27:37
לשון זכר	masculine gender	
לשון חול	the meaning "common, ordinary (not sacred)"	Gen 26:4
לשון טנוף	the meaning "a filthy thing"	Isa 30:22
לשון מסכינו	the meaning "poverty"	Deut 1:21
לשון נקיבה	feminine gender	Gen 31:9
לשון עלייה	the meaning "to go up"	Exod 32:4
לשון ענן	the meaning "clouds"	Jer 10:13
לשון קדש	in sacred language (Hebrew)	Ps 61:8
לשון רבים	plural	Num 13:22
לשון שנאה	the meaning "hating"	Isa 14:21
לשון תגרייא	the meaning "merchants"	Job 40:30
לשון תרגום	in the language of the Targums (Aramaic)	
מאריך	*metheg* (accent). Here called *maʾarîḵ*. Also called *gaʿyāʾ*	2 Kgs 1:2
מגלה	the book of Esther (Literally = "scroll." Although there are other scrolls, "the" scroll is Esther.)	
מגלות	*Megilloth*, the (5) scrolls	Lev 7:9
מדינ̇=מדינחאי	Eastern Babylonian tradition	
מוקדם ומאוחר	with changed order	Dan 4:9

מחליפׄ=מחליפין	those which are otherwise read (i.e., a variant tradition exists)	
מטעׄ=מטעין	leading into error (i.e., this passage tends to generate errors)	
מטעׄ בטעׄ	leading into error of accentuation	
מיחדׄ=מיחדין	peculiar (indicates an unusual use of a word or group of words)	
מילה, מילין	word, words	
ומילה (חדה) ביניהׄ	and (one) word between them	
מ˙ל=מלא	fully written (complete), usually refers to presence of *wāw*	
ומלׄ	and also fully written	
מלכים	the book of Kings	
מלעיל	from above, (indicates accent placed on penultimate syllable)	
מלרע	from below, (indicates accent placed in last syllable)	
מנהׄ=מנהון	from them, of them	
מנוקד, מנוקדין	point(s), pointed	1 Chr 27:1
מנוקדין בתלת	pointed with *s*^{e}*ḡōl* (vowel)	Gen 26:25
מנין	number, the number	Gen 30:30
מנין איש רגלי	the number of foot soldiers	Gen 30:30
מסכינו	poverty	Deut 1:21
מערבׄ=מערבאי	Western Palestinian tradition	
מ״פ=מצע פסוק	middle verse, within a verse	

מפקׄ=מפיק, מפקין	*mappîq* (indicates that the letter in this case is to be pronounced so as to be perceivable by ear)	
מפקׄ א, מפקׄ ה	indicates the letters **א** and ה in this case are to be pronounced so as to be perceivable by ear)	Gen 38:27
מצעא, מיצעא	middle, within	
מקף	*maqqēp̄* (see pp. 5-6)	Gen 30:19
מרעימין	with *šalšelet* (accent)	
משלי	the book of Proverbs	
משנה תורה	the book of Deuteronomy	Exod 20:24
משנׄ	different	Gen 41:26
משנין בטעׄ	with different accent	Ps 55:24
מ״ת=מצע תיבותא	middle word, within a word	1 Sam 18:1
מתאימין	doubly placed	Gen 22:11
דׄ שמואתא מתאימין	four times names are repeated	
מתחלפׄ=מתחלפין	discrepancy (in accentuation, order, etc.)	Deut 8:11
נא	indicates word only occurs (in these places) next to **נא**	
נביאׄ=נביאים	Prophets	
נון רבתי	large letter *nûn*	Num 27:5
נונין זעירין	smaller letters *nûn*	Isa 44:14
נ״ך=נביאים וכתובים	Prophets and Writings	
נסיבין, נסבין	including, with, added	Num 35:15
נסיבׄ ו=נסיבין ו	with *wāw* copulative (*wāw* conjunctive) added	Gen 24:35
נקודׄ=נקודות	puncta extraordinaria (special points)—see p. 3	Gen 16:5

נקיבה	feminine gender	Gen 31:9
סביׄר=סביר, סבירין	*Seberin*, supposed or expected (see p. 15)	
סימן	note, sign, reference chapter, section	
סימן כׄתׄמׄפׄוׄסׄ= הכנעני והחתי והאמרי והפרזי והחוי והיבוסי	reference by which different successions of abbreviations of the names of six peoples indicate different verses of scripture. A list of the combinations and their equivalent is in BHS p. LIII.	see BHS
סימן תׄגׄמׄכׄפׄוׄסׄ= החתי והגרגשי והאמרי והכנעני והפרזי והחוי והיבוסי	reference by which different successions of abbreviations for the names of seven peoples indicate different verses of scripture as shown in BHS p. LIII	Deut 7:1 Neh 9:8 Josh 3:10, 24:11
סימן כׄתׄפׄסׄעׄאׄצׄמׄ= לכנעני החתי הפרזי היבוסי העמני המאבי המצרי והאמרי	reference in which a succession of eight peoples is indicated	Ezra 9:1
צׄפׄקׄ סימן=מצותיו ומשפטיו וחקתיו	reference by which different successions of the abbreviations for three words indicate different verses of scripture as shown on BHS p. LIV	Deut 8:11 Deut 11:1

קׄצׄפׄ סימן =(or צׄקׄפׄ סימן) חקיו ומצותיו ומשפטיו	reference by which different successions of the abbreviations for three words indicate different verses of scripture as shown on BHS p. LIV	Deut 26:17 Deut 30:16 1 Kgs 2:3, 8:58
סימן בׄוׄזׄ מׄיׄםׄ	note derived from key letters from various verses of Numbers 29, so that the letters מׄיׄםׄ refer to a libation of water. This note is fully explained in Yeivin p. 134.	Num 29:33
סימן מׄוׄחׄמׄוׄ=מחלה ונעה חגלה מלכה ותרצה	reference by which different successions of abbreviations for the names of five daughters of Zelophehad indicate different verses of scripture as shown on BHS p. LIV	Num 26:33 Num 27:1 Num 36:11 Josh 17:3
תׄכׄהׄ סימן=תורה: כל המחלה	reference regarding the spelling of כל מחלה in the Pentateuch	Exod 15:26
מׄכׄמׄ סימן=מלכים: כל מחלה	and in the book of Kings	1 Kgs 8:37
דׄומׄ סימן=דברי: הימים וכל מחלה	and in Chronicles	2 Chr 6:28
סיפׄ=סיפרא	book	

סיפ̇ מוגה=סיפרי מוגה	corrected or meticulously written manuscript(s) (which were used as exemplars).	Eccl 7:23
סכום	sum	
סמיכ̇=סמיך, סמיכין	close, closely preceding or following	Lev 6:10
סמיכ̇ לזרקא	preceded by *zarqāʾ*, following *zarqāʾ* (i.e., *s^eḡôltāʾ*)	Gen 37:22
ס״פ=סוף פסוק, סופי פסוקין	end of verses(s)	
ס״ת=סוף תיבותא, סופי תיבותא	end of word(s)	Gen 32:15
עזרא	the book of Ezra and Nehemiah	
עי̇נ, עיני̇נ=עינין, עינינין	context, section	Gen 10:15
עלייה	noun from the verb עלה	Exod 32:4
ענן	clouds	Jer 10:13
פלג̇=פלגין	there are those who might read otherwise (i.e., differences of opinion exist)	Ezek 10:13
פלוני	someone	
אמירה פלוני בלבו	places in which is written ויאמר בלבו or similar	Gen 17:17
פסוק, פסוק̇=פסוק, פסוקין	verse(s)	
פסיק̇, פסיקתא	*pasēq* (see p. 5)	
פרש̇=פרשה	*pārāšāh,* one of 54 sections of the Pentateuch (see p. 2)	Exod 21:7

פשטין פתׄ	indicates syllable is accented by *pašṭāʾ*, *paṯaḥ* vowel to be pronounced	Ps 22:1
פתׄ=פתח	*paṯaḥ* (vowel)	
פתׄ קטן	*s*ᵉ*gōl* (vowel)	Job 21:18
צדה רבתי	large letter *ṣādeh*	Deut 32:4
צורת הבית	description of the temple	Ezek 40:7
קׄ=קרי	*q*ᵉ*rê*, to be read (instead of *k*ᵉ*ṯîḇ*, the written text). See p. 13.	
קדמׄ=קדמא	first, the first	Num 35:15
כספא דקדים	indicates the word **כספא** precedes the word **דהבא**	Dan 2:35
דקדמין לעצים	indicates the word **אבן** precedes the word **עץ**	Lev 14:45
קדש	sacred, holy	Ps 61:8
קהלת	the book of Ecclesiastes	
קׄלׄדׄ	the number 134	Gen 18:3
קמׄ=קמץ	*qāmeṣ* (vowel)	
קמׄ קטן	*ṣērê* (vowel)	Exod 15:11
קרׄ=קרי	*q*ᵉ*rê*, to be read (instead of *k*ᵉ*ṯîḇ*, the written text).	
קריא	holy scripture	
וכל קריא תלופ	in all the scripture a different order	Ruth 4:9
קריבה למיתה	approaching death	Gen 47:29
קריה	town, city, place	
ראש תיבותא	beginning of a word	
ראש תרי עשר	beginning of the book of the Twelve Prophets	
רבי פינחס	Rabbi Pinchas	Ps 144:13
רבים	many, plural	Num 13:22
רבתי	large (of large letters)	Num 27:5
נון רבתי	large letter *nûn*	Num 27:5

צדה רבתי	large letter *ṣādeh*	Deut 32:4
ר״פ=ראש פסוק, ריש פסוקא, ראשי פסוקין, רישי פסוקין	beginning of verse(s)	
רפי׳=רפי, רפין	*rāp̄eh* (see p. 7)	
ר״ת=ראש תיבותא	beginning of a word	
שאה	storm	
שאר	others, the rest	Exod 17:8
שבט	family, tribe	Num 2:14
שינה	sleep	Jer 51:39
שיר השירים	the book of Song of Songs	
שלֹשׁ=שלשה	three	
שלֹשׁ ספרים	the Three Books (Psalms, Job, Proverbs)	
שם	name	
שם אִיתְ	woman's name	Isa 6:6
שם אֹנש	man's name	Exod 29:40
שם באר	name of a well	Gen 26:33
שם ברנש	man's name	Exod 30:13
שם קריה	name of a city	Josh 15:24
שם תרגום	word from a Targum (see Mynatt pp. 117-118)	Exod 16:13
שמואל	the book of Samuel	
שמואתא מתאימין	name repeated	Gen 22:11
שמיעה לקול	(with) the meaning to hear a voice (to obey)	Gen 3:17
שמשון	Samson	Gen 42:24
שנאה	enmity	Isa 14:21
שפטים	the book of Judges	
תְּדְמְּקְ=תרי עשר, דברי הימים, משלי, קהלת	the book of Twelve Prophets, Chronicles, Proverbs and Ecclesiastes	Ps 1:6

תור֯=תורה	the Pentateuch	
תיבותא	word	
תלויות	raised (of raised letters)	Judg 18:30
תלים, תהלים	the book of Psalms	
תלת	three, *s*^{e}*ḡōl* (which is three dots)	Gen 26:25
מנוקדין בתלת	pointed with *s*^{e}*ḡōl* (vowel)	Gen 26:25
תנופ֯=תנופה	activity of sacrifices in the presence of God (see BDB p. 632)	Isa 33:20
תנינ֯=תנינא	second	
תרגום	Targum, language of the Targum (Aramaic)	
תר֯י=תרי, תרין, תרתי, תרתין	two	
תרי֯ טעמ֯	two accents	2 Kgs 17:13
תרי֯ לישנ֯	two meanings	Exod 5:18
כת֯ מילה חדה וקר֯ תרי֯	written as one word but read as two	Gen 30:11
כת֯ תרי֯ ו	written with double letter *wāw*	Exod 37:8
תרי עשר	the book of the Twelve Prophets	

7
TRANSLITERATION OF NAMES AND TERMS

Hebrew or Aramaic	**Lambdin Transliteration**	**Other names and spellings**
אַזְלָא	*ʾazlāʾ*	*azla*
אָלֶף	*ʾālep̄*	*aleph*
אַתְנָח	*ʾaṯnāḥ*	*athnach, etnachta*
בֵּית	*bêṯ*	*beth, bet*
גָּדוֹל	*gāḏôl*	*gadol*, great
גְּדוֹלָה	*g^{e}ḏôlāh*	*gedolah*, great
גַּלְגַּל	*galgal*	
גִּמֶל	*gîmel*	*gimel, gimmel*
גַּעְיָא	*gaʿyāʾ*	*gaʿya, metheg, maʾarikh*
גֶּרֶשׁ	*gereš*	*geresh*
גֵּרְשַׁיִם	*gēr$^{\breve{e}}$šayim*	*gerashayim*
דָּגֵשׁ	*dāḡēš*	*dagesh, daghesh*
דְּחִי	*d^{e}ḥî*	*dehi, deḥi*

Hebrew or Aramaic	**Lambdin Transliteration**	**Other names and spellings**
דָּלֶת	*dāleṯ*	*dalet, daled, daleth*
דַּרְגָּא	*dargāʾ*	*darga*
הֵא	*hēʾ*	*hey, heh*
הִירֶק	*hîreq*	*ḥirik, chireq*
וָו	*wāw*	*waw, vav*
זַיִן	*zayin*	*zayin*
זָקֵף	*zāqēp̄*	*zaqeph, zaqef*
זַרְקָא	*zarqāʾ*	*zarqa*
חָטוּף	*ḥāṭûp̄*	*ḥatuf, chatuf*
חָטֵף	*ḥāṭēp̄*	*ḥatef, ḥataf*
חִירֶק	*ḥîreq*	*hirik, chireq*
חֵית	*ḥēṯ*	*chet, heth*
חֹלֶם	*ḥōlem*	*holem, cholem, cholam*
טֵית	*ṭēṯ*	*tet*
טִפְּחָה	*ṭip̄ḥāh*	*tifcha*
טַרְחָא	*ṭarḥāʾ*	*tarcha*
יוֹד	*yôḏ*	*yod*
יְתִיב	*y*^{e}*ṯîḇ*	*yetiv, yethib*
כַּף	*kap̄*	*kaf*
כְּפוּלָה	*ḵ*^{e}*p̄ûlāh*	*kefulah*, double
כְּתִיב	*k*^{e}*ṯîḇ*	*kethib, ketiv*
לְגַרְמֵהּ	*l*^{e}*ḡarmeh*	
לָמֶד	*lāmeḏ*	*lamed*

Hebrew or Aramaic	Lambdin Transliteration	Other names and spellings
מְאַיְּלָא	*mᵉayyᵉlaʾ*	*mayela*
מַאֲרִיךְ	*maʾarîḵ*	*gaʿya, metheg*
מֻגְרָשׁ	*muḡrāš*	*mugrash*
מַהְפַּךְ	*mahpaḵ*	*mᵉhuppak*
מוּנַח	*mûnaḥ*	*munach*
מֵירְכָא	*mêrᵉḵāʾ*	*merka, mercha*
מֵם	*mēm*	*mem*
מַפִּיק	*mappîq*	
מַקֵּף	*maqqēp̄*	*maqqef*
מֶתֶג	*meṯeḡ*	*metheg*
נוּן	*nûn*	*nun*
סְבִיר	*sᵉḇîr*	*sebir, seberin* (pl)
סְגֹל	*sᵉḡōl*	*segol*
סְגוֹלְתָּא	*sᵉḡôltāʾ*	*segolta*
סֵדֶר	*sēḏer*	*seder, sedarim* (pl)
סוֹף	*sôp̄*	*sof, soph*
סִלּוּק	*sillûq*	*silluq*
סָמֶךְ	*sameḵ*	*samek, samech*
סְתוּמָא	*sᵉṯûmāʾ*	*setuma*
עוֹלֶה וְיוֹרֵד	*ʿôleh wᵉyôrēḏ*	*ole we-yored*
עַיִן	*ʿayin*	*ayin*
עִלּוּי	*ʿillûy*	*illuy*
פֵּה (or פֵּא)	*pēh*	*pey, pē*

Hebrew or Aramaic	Lambdin Transliteration	Other names and spellings
פָּזֵר	*pāzēr*	*pazer*
פַּסֵק (or פַּסִיק)	*pasēq*	*pasîq*
פָּסוּק	*pāsûq*	
פָּרָשָׁה	*pārāšāh*	*parashah, parashoth* (pl)
פַּתַח	*paṯaḥ*	*patach, pathach*
צָדֵה (צָדִי, צָדֵי)	*ṣāḏeh*	*tsade, tzadi*
צִנּוֹר	*ṣinnôr*	*tsinnor*
צִנּוֹרִית	*ṣinnôrîṯ*	*tsinnorith*
צֵרֵי	*ṣērê*	*sere, tsere, tzere*
קִבּוּץ	*qibbûṣ*	*qibbuts, kubbutz*
קוֹף	*qôp̄*	*qōp̄, qof, kof*
קָטֹן	*qāṭōn*	*qaton, qatan*, small
קְטַנָּה	*q*^{e}*ṭannāh*	*qetanna*, small
קָמֶץ	*qāmeṣ*	*qamets, kamatz katan*
קְרֵי	*q*^{e}*rê*	*qere*
רְבִיעַ	*r*^{e}*ḇî*^{a}*ʿ*	*rebia, revia*
רֵישׁ (רֵשׁ)	*rêš*	*resh*
רָפֶה	*rāp̄eh*	*raphe*
שִׂין	*śîn*	*sin*
שְׁוָא	*š*^{e}*wāʾ*	*shewa, sheva, sh*^{e}*wa*
שׁוּרֶק	*šûrĕq*	*shureq, shurek, shuruk*

Hebrew or Aramaic	**Lambdin Transliteration**	**Other names and spellings**
שִׁין	*šîn*	*shin*
שַׁלְשֶׁלֶת	*šalšeleṯ*	*shalshelet, shalsheleth*
תְּבִיר	*t*^{e}*ḇîr*	*tebir, tevir*
תְּלִישָׁא	*t*^{e}*lîšāʾ*	*telisha*
תָּו	*tāw*	*taw, tav*

ABBREVIATED BIBLIOGRAPHY

BDB: Brown, Driver and Briggs, *A Hebrew and English Lexicon of the Old Testament*. Oxford: Clarendon, 1907 (corrected impression 1952).

BHK: Kittel, R., et al, *Biblia Hebraica*. Stuttgart: Privileg. Wurtt. Bibelanstalt, 1937.

BHS: Elliger, K., et al, *Biblia Hebraica Stuttgartensia*. Stuttgart: Deutsche Bibelgesellschaft, 1967/1977.

Ginsberg, C.D., *Introduction to the Massoretic-Critical Edition of the Hebrew Bible*. New York: Ktav, 1966. Originally published 1897.

Haïk-Vantoura, Suzanne H., *The Music of the Bible Revealed*. Translated by Dennis Weber, edited by John Wheeler. Berkeley: BIBAL Press, 1991

Herzog, A. "Masoretic Accents" in *Encyclopaedia Judaica*. Jerusalem: Keter, 1972.

Kautzsch, E., ed. *Gesenius' Hebrew Grammar*. Translated by A. E. Cowley. Oxford: Clarendon, 1910/1985.

Lambdin, Thomas O., *Introduction to Biblical Hebrew*. New York: Scribners, 1971.

Mynatt, Daniel S., *The Sub Loco Notes of the Torah of Biblia Hebraica Stuttgartensia*. BIBAL Dissertation Series 2. N. Richland Hills, TX: BIBAL Press, 1995.

Roberts, Bleddyn J., *The Old Testament Text and Versions*. Cardiff: University of Wales, 1951.

Rüger, H.P., *An English Key to the Latin Words and Abbreviations and the Symbols of Biblia Hebraica Stuttgartensia*. Stuttgart: German Bible Society, 1985.

Weil, Gerard E. *Massorah Gedolah*. Vol. 1. Rome: Biblical Institute Press, 1971.

Werner, E. "Masoretic Accents" in *Interpreter's Dictionary of the Bible*, Vol III. New York: Abingdon, 1962.

Wickes, W. *Two Treatises on the Accentuation of the Old Testament*. New York: Ktav, 1970. Originally published in 1881 and 1887.

Wonneberger, R. *Understanding BHS: A Manual for the Users of Biblia Hebraica Stuttgartensia*. Rome: Biblical Institute Press, 1984.

Würthwein, E. *The Text of the Old Testament*. Translated by E. F. Rhodes. Grand Rapids: Eerdmans, 1979.

Yeivin, I. *Introduction to the Tiberian Masorah*. Translated by E. J. Revell. Missoula, Montana: Scholars, 1980.

ʾālep̄ 39, 52
ʾaṯnāḥ 25, 27–8, 31, 33–5, 38–9, 52
ʾazlāʾ 29–31, 34, 52
ʿayin 4, 54
ʿillûy 34, 54
ʿôleh wᵉyôrēḏ 33, 54
abbreviations 15
accents 25–36, 38, 40–3, 45, 51
Aquila 22
Arabic 22
Aramaic 12, 38–9, 43, 51
Armenian 22
asteriscus 23
Babylon 9
Babylonian tradition 2, 9
Ben Asher 10, 19, 38
Ben Chayim 10, 18
Ben Jacob 18
Ben Naphtali 10, 38
bêṯ 52
cantillation 25, 35–6
chapters, division into 1
closed paragraph 1
codex 18–9
Codex Leningradensis 1, 6–7, 11–2, 18–9
colophon 18–9
conjunctive accents 6, 25–7, 31, 34
conjunctive *wāw* 45
construct state 6
Coptic 22
copulative *wāw* 45
critical apparatus 13, 15–24
dagesh 7, 39, 52
dāleṯ 4, 53
dargāʾ 29–31, 53
defective spelling 13, 40
dᵉḥî 34, 52
disjunctive 25–8, 33
divine name 13, 37
Eastern tradition 9, 43
editors, BHS 19–20, 22
Ethiopic 22
exemplars 48
Ezra 8
festal scrolls 36, 40
gāḏôl 29, 31, 33–4, 52
galgal 31, 34, 52
gaʿyāʾ 6, 38, 43, 52, 54
gᵉḏôlāh 12, 31–3, 52
gereš 30, 38, 52
gērᵉšayim 30, 52
Gesenius 5–6, 27
gîmel 52
Ginsberg 3, 16
Hagiographa 42
Haïk-Vantoura 36
hēʾ 53
hexapla 23–4
hîreq 6, 53
ḥāṭēp̄ 40, 53
ḥāṭûp̄ 6, 53
ḥēṯ 53
ḥîreq 53
ḥōlem 53
inverted *nûn* 3
Isaac 41
itture sopherim 15–6
kap̄ 53
kᵉp̄ûlāh 31, 53
kᵉṯîḇ 13–4, 16, 24, 42, 49, 53
lāmeḏ 53
large letters 4, 49
lᵉḡarmeh 5, 30, 34, 42, 53
liturgical cycle 2
maʾarîḵ 6, 43, 52, 54
mahpaḵ 31, 54
Manasseh 4
mappîq 7, 39, 45, 54
maqqēp̄ 5–6, 19, 25, 35, 45, 54
mâyᵉlāʾ 31
masora 2, 8–18, 42
masora finalis 10
masora magna 10–2, 16
masora marginalis 11
masora parva 11–6, 32, 37, 42
masoretes 8–11, 13, 15, 18, 36
Masoretic Text 22
mᵉʾayyᵉlāʾ 31, 54
Megilloth 43
mᵉhuppāḵ 30–1, 34–5, 54
mēm 54
mêrᵉkāʾ 27–31, 34–5, 54
merka 31, 34, 54
metheg 6, 25, 35, 38, 40, 43, 52, 54
metobelus 23
mid-point 4, 11, 40
Mishnah 8
Moses 4
muḡrāš 33, 54
mûnaḥ 27–31, 34, 54
musical motives 35
musical value 25, 29–30
Mynatt 4, 14, 16–7, 50
nakdanim 9
numbers 14, 37, 39
nûn 3–4, 39, 45, 49, 54
obelus 23–4
Old Latin 22
open paragraph 1
Origen 23
Palestinian tradition 1, 9
paragogic 41

paragraphs · · · · · · 1
pārāšāh · · · 2, 48, 55
pasēq · · · · 5, 25, 30, 33–5, 48, 55
pasîq · · · · · · · · 5
pāsûq · · · · · · 1, 55
paštāʾ · · · · 30–1, 49
pataḥ · · · · 39, 49, 55
pausal forms · · · · 28
pāzēr · · · · 31, 34, 55
Pentateuch · · 2, 35–7, 40–2, 47–8, 51
pericopes · · · · 42, 48
perpetual *qᵉrê* · · 13–4
pᵉṯûḥāʾ · · · · · · · 1
postpositive · · · · 27, 29–31, 33
prepositive 30–1, 34, 41
Prophets · · · · 36, 45
puncta extraordinaria 3, 45
qāmeṣ · · 6, 39, 49, 55
qarnê pārāh · · · · 31
qāṭan · · · · · 28, 31
qāṭōn · 28–9, 31, 33, 55
qᵉrê · · · 12–4, 16, 24, 49, 55
qᵉṭannāh · · 12, 29–33, 35, 55
qibbûṣ · · · · · · · 55
qôp̄ · · · · · · 13, 55
Rabbi Pinchas · · · 49
Rabbinic Bible · · · 18
raised letters · · 4–5, 51
rāp̄eh · · · · 7, 50, 55
rᵉḇîaʿ · 29–31, 33–4, 55
rêš · · · · · · · · · 55
Roberts · · · · · · · 15
Rüger · · · · 20, 22–3
Sahidic · · · · · · · 22
Samaritan Pentateuch 20, 22
samek · · · · · · · 54
Samson · · · · · 42, 50
scribal corrections 15, 24
scribal omissions · · 15
scribes 3–4, 9, 11, 15–6
scrolls · · · · · 18, 43
seberin · · · 15, 24, 46
second Rabbinic Bible 18
sᵉḇîr · · · · · · · · 54
sᵉdārîm · · 1–2, 11, 54
sᵉḡōl · · 44, 49, 51, 54
sᵉḡōltāʾ 28–9, 40, 48, 54
semantic division · · 25
semantic value · 29–30
Septuagint · · 20, 22–4
servi · · · 26–31, 33–4
sᵉṯûmāʾ · · · · · 1, 54
sillûq · 27–8, 31, 33, 54
small letters · · · · · 4
sôp̄ · · · · · · · · · 54
sôp̄ pāsûq · · · · · · 1
sopherim · · · · · 9, 16
special points · · 3, 45
sub loco · · · · · · 17
symbols · · · · · 20–1
Symmachus · · · · 22
Syriac · · · · · · · · 22
ṣāḏeh · · · · 49–50, 55
ṣērê · · · · · · · · 55
ṣinnôr · · 33–4, 40, 55
ṣinnôrîṯ · 33, 35, 40, 55
śîn · · · · · · · · · 55
šalšeleṯ · · · · 29, 33, 35, 45, 56
šᵉwāʾ · · · · · · · · 55
šîn · · · · · · · · 4, 56
šûrĕq · · · · · · · · 55
Targum(s) · · · 18, 22, 43, 50–1
tāw · · · · · · · · · 56
tᵉḇîr · · · 26, 30–1, 56
tᵉlîšāʾ · · 12, 29–32, 56
temple · · · · · · · 49
tetragrammaton · · 41
text criticism · · · · 22
textual variants · · · 13
textus receptus · · 9, 18
Theodotion · · · · · 22
Three Books 25, 32–4, 36, 50
Tiberian tradition 9–10, 18, 38
tiqqune sopherim 15, 24
Torah · · · · · · 11, 17
transliteration · · · 52
twelve prophets 49–51
Twenty-One Books 25, 27–9, 31–3, 35
ṭarḥāʾ · · · · · 34, 53
ṭip̄ḥāh · · · 27–31, 53
unique words · · 14, 42
unusual letters · · · · 3
versions · · · · 20, 22
vowel points · · · · 13
Vulgate · · · · · · 22
wāw · · 4, 15–6, 44–5, 51, 53
Western tradition 9, 44
Wickes · · · · · 27, 32
Wonneberger · · 20, 23
Writings · · · · 42, 45
Würthwein · · · 16, 22
Yeivin 3–7, 15–6, 27, 32, 47
yeraḥ · · · · · · 31, 34
yᵉṯîḇ · · · · · · 30, 53
yôḏ · · · · · · · · · 53
zāqēp̄ · · 27–30, 39, 53
zayin · · · · · · · · 53
zarqāʾ · 29–31, 33, 40, 48, 53
Zelophehad · · · · 47

An English Key

to the Latin Words and Abbreviations
and the Symbols of
BIBLIA HEBRAICA STUTTGARTENSIA
by Prof. Dr. Hans Peter Rüger

A

A

a, ab — from Nu 32,32[c]
abbreviatio, onis — abbreviation Jos 15, 49[a]
abbreviatum — abbreviated Ex 36, 8[b]
aberratio oculi — visual error Nu 9, 23[a-a]
abhinc — hence Ex 36, 8[b]
abiit — he has departed 2 Ch 21, 20[b-b]
abs(olutus) — absolute Nu 8, 12[a]
abstractum, i — abstract Jer 7, 32[a]
absumuntur — they are ruined Ps 37, 20[a-a]
abundantia — abundance Ps 72, 16[a]
abundavit — he has abounded Jes 57, 9[a]
ac — and, and besides; to Lv 16, 10[a]; 2S 10, 6[b]
acc(entus, us) — accent Gn 35, 22[a-a]
acc(usativus) — accusative Lv 27, 31[a]
accusavit — he has accused Jes 41, 27[b]
act(ivum) — active Ex 31, 15[a]
acuta, ae — acute, accented Lv 18, 28[a]
ad — to Gn 4, 7[b-b]
adde — add Nu 24, 24[g-g]
addit — it adds Neh 9, 10[a]
additamentum, i — addition 2Ch 12, 11[a]
add(itum) — added Gn 2, 19[c-c]

A A

addunt — they add Jos 22, 34[b]
adjunget — it will join Jer 33, 13[a-a]
admodum — very Ex 36, 8[b]
adverbialis — adverbial Da 11, 7[c]
aeg(yptiacus, a, um; e) — (in) Egyptian Jos 15, 9[a-a]
aenus, a, um — brazen 1Ch 18, 8[g]
aequalitas — equality Ez 48, 2-7[a-a]
aequavit — he has compared Jer 48, 6[b]
aes — copper, bronze Jdc 5, 14[d]
aeth(iopicus, a, um; e) — (in) Ethiopic 1S 19, 20[b]
aeva — generations Ps 90, 5[a]
afflictans, antis — vexing Jer 46, 16[e]
agnus — lamb Jes 5, 17[d]
agri, orum — fields Jer 39, 10[a]
akk(adicus, a, um; e) — (in) Akkadian Jos 13, 3[a]
alias — elsewhere 2R 14, 29[a]
alibi — elsewhere 2S 2, 7[b]
aliena — another's, foreign Lv 18, 21[b]
aliqui — some Lv 18, 11[a]
aliquot — some 2S 17, 8b
alit(er) — otherwise Ex 4, 25[a-a]
al(ius, a, um; ii, ae, a) — other(s) Gn 32, 18[a]
altare, is — altar Jos 22, 34[b]
alter, a, um — another, the other Hi 16, 20[a-a]
alterutrum — either, one of two 1R 5, 14[b]
altus — high Jes 11, 11[a]
amicus — friend Jes 44, 28[a]
amplius — more Ex 20, 19[a-a]
an — or Ez 1, 8[b-b]
angeli, orum — angels Ps 89, 7[a]
angulus, i — angle, corner Ez 8, 3[c]
anhelare — to pant Dt 33, 21[a]
animadversio — attention Hi 4, 20[a]

A A

animalia — animals Ps 50, 11[b]
annus — year Nu 20, 1[a]
ante — before Gn 49, 26[a-a]
antea — before this Jdc 2, 16[a]
aperiens — opening Ex 13, 13[a]
aperte — openly Ps 12, 6[d-d]
apertio — opening Hab 2, 3[a]
apertus — open Nu 24, 3[b]
apud — at, with Jdc 20, 27[a-a]
aquae, arum — waters Jer 51, 12[a-a]
aquosi — abounding in water Jer 31, 40[d]
arab(icus, a, um; e) — (in) Arabic Nu 16, 1[a]
aram(aicus, a, um; e) — (in) Aramaic Gn 15, 2[a-a]
aranea — cobweb Ps 90, 9[d]
arbor, oris — tree Jes 44, 4[a]
art(iculus) — article Est 2, 14[a]
ascensus, us — ascent 2Ch 9, 4[c]
asseritur — it is delivered Jer 25, 14[c]
assimilatum — assimilated Da 4, 14[b]
ast(eriscus, i) — asterisk Dt 4, 21[e]
at — but Da 2, 5[a]
Atbaš — a device in which a word is spelled by substitution of the last letter of the alphabet for the first, the next to last for the second, etc.; hence the name aleph-taw-beth-shin Jer 25, 25[a]
attulit — he has brought Jes 61, 6[a]
auctus — augmented Hab 3, 2[a]
aucupes — fowlers Jer 5, 26[a-a]
audacia — courage Da 3, 29[a]
auster, tri — south Ps 107, 3[c]
aut — or; aut . . . aut — either . . . or Nu 15, 28[a]; 15, 29[a]
auxiliator — helper Ps 62, 8[b]
aversio, onis — turning away Jer 31, 19[a]
aves, ium — birds Dt 14, 12[a]

B B

bab(ylonicus, a, um) — Babylonian Jes 52, 14[c]
bellator — warrior Ex 15, 3[b]
bene — well 2Ch 4, 2[a-a]
benedixit — he has blessed 1R 5, 15[c]
bestia — beast Hos 9, 13[a-a]
bis — twice Ex 6, 2[a]
bonum — good 2Ch 3, 6[a]
boves — oxen, bulls 1Ch 18, 8[g]
brachium — arm Jes 63, 5[c]
brevis — short Hi 8, 14[b]
brevius — shorter Dt 29, 14[a]

C C

campus, i — field Jer 31, 40[d]
canticum — song Da 3, 23[a]
capella — Capella (astronomy) Am 5, 9[d]
capillus, i — hair of the head Jes 57, 9[b]
captivitas — captivity Thr 1, 20[a-a]
castella — castles, citadels 2S 20, 14[a]
castigatio — punishment Hi 36, 18[b]
catena, ae — chain, fetters Ps 66, 11[b]
cave — beware of Hi 36, 18[a]
cecidit — it has fallen Ps 55, 5[a]
celeriter — quickly Ex 12, 21[b-b]
celerius — quicker Hi 4, 19[a]
cet(eri, ae, a) — the others, the rest 1S 1, 15[a]
cf — confer — compare Gn 1, 6[a]
cj — conjunge, conjungit, conjungunt — connect, it connects, they connect Gn 1, 11[a-a]
clandestina — hidden 2R 11, 6[b]
clemens — merciful Jes 9, 16[a]
codd — codices — codices, ancient manuscripts Lv 18, 11[a]
cod(ex) — codex, ancient manuscript Gn 18, 21[a]
cogitare, cogitaverunt —to consider, they have considered Hi 21, 27[a]

collectivum — collective Gn 40, 10[b]
collocabit — he will place Da 11, 39[a]
commeatus, us — provisions Jes 61, 6[a]
commutatum, commutavit —changed, it has exchanged 2Ch 25, 23[a-a]
compl(ures) — several Mal 2, 15[c]
compone — arrange Jer 40, 1[a]
concretum — concrete Jer 7, 32[a]
confisus est — he has trusted in Prv 18, 10[a]
confusus, a, um — confused Ex 36, 8[b]
conjg — conjungendum — to be connected Neh 12, 25[b]
conservatus, i — preserved Da 7, 11[a-a]
consilia — counsels Prv 31, 3[c]
constituit — he has appointed 1Ch 26, 1[b]
constructio — construction Hi 31, 11[c-c]
consuetudo, inis — habit 2S 2, 27[a]
contaminatum — contaminated Jos 8, 33[c]
contempores — despisers, contemners Sach 9, 1[c-c]
contendo — I contend, I dispute Hi 16, 20[a-a]
contentio, onis — contest, fight Ps 55, 19[c]
contextus, us — context Da 7, 11[a-a]
continent — they contain Prv 25, 20[a-a]
continuantur, continuatur — they are joined, it is joined Jer 19, 2[a-a]
contra — against Nu 31, 16[b-b]
contrarium — contrary Nu 12, 1[b-b]
conventus, us — meeting, assembly Da 6, 7[a]
conservatio, onis — conversation
copiae, arum — military forces Da 11, 6[b]
cop(ula, ae) — copula Ex 1, 1[a]
coram — in the presence of Ps 18, 41[a-a]
cornu — horn Ex 19, 13[a-a]
correctio — correction Hi 1, 5[a]
corr(ectus, a, um) — corrected 2Ch 16, 5[a]
corrigens — correcting Ez 43, 11[d-d]

C C

corruptum — corrupt 1Ch 27, 4[b-b]
cp — caput, itis — chapter Gn 32, 2[a]
crrp — corruptus, a, um — corrupt Ex 14, 9[a]
crudeles — cruel Nu 21, 6[a]
cs — causaā — on account of Jer 4, 8[a]
cstr — constructus — construct Ps 75, 7[d]
c(um) — with Gn 1, 11[a-a]
cum — when Ex 19, 13[a-a]
curat — he takes care of Hi 20, 20[a-a]
curculio — weevil Jes 41, 14[a]
cursus — running Hi 4, 20[a]
custodia — watch Na 2, 2[c]
custos, odis — keeper, watchman Ps 141, 3[a]

D D

dare, dat — to give, it gives Dt 6, 3[d]
de — from, by reason of Nu 31, 18[a]
dedisti — you have given Ps 8, 2[a-a]
deest — it is missing Nu 13, 7[a-a]
defatigare — to fatigue, to tire Prv 6, 3[c]
deficiens, entis — missing Esr 10, 36[a]
deficient — they will fail Da 12, 4[a]
deformare — to deform Prv 28, 12[b]
deliciae, arum — delight Jer 6, 2[a-a]
delirium — silliness Ps 31, 19[a]
deminutio — diminution, decrease Hag 2, 19[a]
deprecari — to deprecate, to pray against Jes 47, 11[b]
descendant — let them descend Ps 31, 18[a]
descriptio, onis — description Ez 40, 7/8/9[b]
desiderare — to desire Dt 33, 21[a]
desideratus — missed 2Ch 21, 20[b-b]
desiit — it left off, it ceased Hos 7, 16[b-b]
destinatus — destined Hi 15, 22[a]
desunt — they are missing Ex 2, 1[a]

D D

detentus — detained Ps 88, 9[b]
detrahere — to take off Neh 3, 15[d]
deus — god Ps 4, 2[b]
dicteria, iorum — witticisms Hi 17, 6[a]
dies — day Sach 1, 1[a]
differt — it differs Da 3, 31[a]
dilecta — loved Jer 49, 4[b]
direxit — he has led Jes 60, 4[a]
distinctius — more distinctly 1Ch 10, 7[a]
diu — a long while Ps 35, 15[a]
divinum — divine Dt 33, 27[e]
divisit — he has separated Nu 16, 1[a]
divulgavit — he has divulged Hi 33, 27[a]
dl — dele, delendus, a , um — delete, to be deleted Gn 1, 11[c]
doce — teach Ps 119, 29[a]
doctrina, ae — instruction Prv 22, 18[a]
domicilium — dwelling 1Ch 4, 41[b]
domina, ae — lady, mistress Jer 31, 22[b-b]
dominabuntur — they will rule Ob 20[a-a]
dominus, i — lord Nu 31, 16[b-b]
domus — house Ps 46, 5[b]
dttg — dittographice — by dittography Gn 20, 4[b-b]
du(alis) — dual Dt 2, 7[c]
dub(ius, a, um) — doubtful Nu 18, 29[b-b]
ducunt — they derive Jer 44, 10[a]
duodecies — twelve times Jos 10, 24[e]
dupl(ex, icis) — double Gn 35, 22[a-a]
dupl(um) — doublet Gn 18, 6[a]
durus — hard Jer 17, 9[a]
dux, ducis — leader 1Ch 27, 4[b-b]
dysenteria — dysentery Mi 6, 14[c]

E E

e, ex — out of, from Gn 16, 11[a]
ecce — behold Ex 17, 16[a]
egerunt, egit — they have acted, he has acted Nu 16, 1[a]
egredientur — they will march out Nu 24, 24[a]
eiciendum — to be dislocated Prv 22, 17[b-b]
elationes — elevations Hi 36, 29[b]
electi, orum — chosen Nu 31, 5[a]
elige — choose Ps 37, 37[b]
emendatus — emended Sach 5, 6[a-a]
emissarius — emissary Jes 39, 1[b]
emphaticum — emphatic Hi 11, 11[a]
en — behold Ex 2, 9[a]
encliticum — enclitic Jdc 3, 2[b]
energicus, a, um — energic Jdc 5, 26[a]
eques, itis — rider Ps 33, 17[a]
equi — horses Sach 6, 6[a-a]
erasum — erased 2S 10, 16[a]
erat — it was Nu 27, 11[d]
erimus — we will be Ps 20, 8[b]
error, oris — error Hi 4, 18[a]
es, esse, est — you are, to be, he, she, it is
et — and; et . . . et — both . . . and Gn 1, 6[a]; Jer 43, 13[a-a]
etc — et cetera — and so forth Lv 1, 7[a-a]
etiam — also Dt 30, 16[c]
etsi — although 1Ch 28, 7[a-a]
euphemismus — euphemism Hi 1, 5[a]
exalti — raised Ps 56, 3[c-c]
exarescere — to dry up Hi 5, 3[a]
exaudivisti — you have heard Ps 38, 16[a-a]
exc — exciderunt, excidisse, excidit — they have dropped out, to have dropped out, it has dropped out Ex 2, 25[a]
excepto — except Dt 14, 12[a]
excipit — it continues Hos 2, 19[a]

E E

excitantes, excitaverunt — causing, they have caused Ps 140, 3[b]
exegesis, eos — exegesis Dt 32, 1[a]
exemplum, i — example 1S 15, 4[a]
exercitus — army 2R 25, 11[b]
explicitum — explained 2S 13, 39[a]
expone — make known Nu 25, 4[c]
exstat — it exists Ex 36, 8[b]
exsultare — to exult Hi 31, 29[a]
extendere — to extend, to stretch out Ps 68, 32[c-c]
extr(aordinarius, a, um) — extraordinary Gn 16, 5[a]

F F

facilior — easier Jos 11, 2[a]
false — falsely Jos 1, 1[c]
falso — falsely Nu 25, 8[a-a]
falsum — false Jer 21, 13[d]
fecit — he has made Ps 105, 20[a-a]
f(emininus, a, um) — feminine Gn 38, 2[a]
fem(ininus, a, um) — feminine Jes 49, 15[a]
fere — nearly, almost Jos 16, 10[a]
fides — loyalty Ps 17, 15[b]
fiducia — trust, confidence Ps 84, 6[c]
filius, ii — son 1Ch 7, 15[c]
finire — to end Hi 27, 8[a]
fin(is, is) — end Ex 36, 8[b]
finit(um) — finite Jes 46, 1[a]
firmus — firm, strong Jes 44, 12[c]
flagitum — crime Ps 36, 2[b-b]
fluvius, ii — river Hi 20, 28[b]
follis — pair of bellows Prv 26, 21[a]
fontes — sources Hi 28, 11[a-a]
forma — form Gn 16, 11[a]
fortis, e — strong Ps 20, 8[b]
fortitudo — strength Nu 23, 22[c]

F F

fossa — ditch, trench Da 9, 25[c]
fovea, ae — pit Ps 17, 14[e]
fragmentum — fragment Sach 7, 7[a]
franges — you will break Ps 18, 41[a-a]
frater, tris — brother Hi 20, 20[a-a]
fremitus — roaring Hi 4, 14[a]
frequentavit — he has frequented Jes 44, 9[b]
frt — fortasse — perhaps Gn 1, 21[a]
fugiant — they flee Ps 60, 6[c]
fui, fuit — I have been, he has been Da 10, 13[a-a]
fulge — shine forth Ps 35, 3[a]
furor — fury, rage Ps 81, 16[b]

G G

gemma — jewel Prv 26, 8[b]
generatim — generally Nu 7, 19[a]-23[a]
genitor, oris — begetter, father 1Ch 8, 7[b]
genus — kind Jes 40, 20[a]
gladius, ii — sword Ps 17, 13[a]
gloria, ae — glory Ps 8, 3[a]
gl(ossa) — gloss Gn 4, 7[b-b]
glossator — glossator Jer 48, 6[b]
graece — in Greek 1Ch 27, 33[a]

H H

hab(ent, et) — they have, they esteem; it has Ex 20, 17[a]
habita — inhabit, live Ps 11, 1[b]
habitaculum, i — dwelling Ps 46, 5[b]
hasta, ae — spear, lance Ps 35, 3[a]
hebr(aicus, a, um; e) — (in) Hebrew Dt 17, 9[a-a]
hemist(ichus) — hemistich Jes 9, 5[c]
hic, haec, hoc; hi, hae, haec — this; these Ps 147, 8[a]
hic — here Gn 4, 8[a]
hinc — hence Hos 5, 15[b]
homark — homoioarcton Gn 31, 18[a-a]

H
H

homines — men Nu 24, 17[h]
homtel — homoioteleuton Lv 1, 8[b-b]
honor — honor Prv 5, 9[b]
hora, ae — hour Esr 9, 4[b-b]
hostes — enemies Ps 9, 7[b]
hpgr — haplographice — by haplography Gn 41, 31[a]
hpleg — hapax legomenon Jdc 3, 23[a]
huc — hither Gn 1, 6[a]
humulis — simple Hi 12, 18[a]

I
I

iam — already Dt 33, 2[c]
ibi — there 2Ch 5, 10[b]
ibidem — in the same place Jer 39, 8[a]
id(em) — the same Nu 1, 9[a]
idem, eadem, idem — the same 1R 8, 16[b]
ignis — fire Hi 18, 15[a-a]
imbres — showers of rain Na 1, 12[a-a]
immergite — immerse Jer 51, 12[a-a]
impar — unequal 2S 17, 8[b]
imp(erativus) — imperative Dt 2, 4[b-b]
imperia — empires Ps 47, 10[c]
impetus — assault, attack Jes 14, 31[b]
impf — imperfectum — imperfect 1S 2, 28[a]
improbabiliter — improbably 2S 18, 14[b]
impudice — shamelessly Nu 16, 1[a]
in — in, into Gn 20, 16[b-b]
incendere — to set fire to Nu 21, 14[b]
inc(ertus, a, um) — uncertain, doubtful Lv 21, 4[a]
incip(it, iunt) — it begins, they begin Gn 32, 2[a]
incolae — inhabitants 1Ch 2, 55[a]
increpatio — rebuke Ps 30, 6[a]
inde — thence Da 3, 31[a]
index — proof Jer 29, 24[a-a]

I I

inf(initivus) — infinitive Lv 14, 43[c]
infirmitas — infirmity, weakness Mi 6, 14[c]
infodi — I have dug in Neh 13, 25[b]
iniquus — unjust Ps 36, 2[b-b]
init(ium) — beginning Nu17, 2/3[e-e]
iniuste — unjustly Nu 31, 16[b-b]
inscriptio, onis -inscription Ps 119, 130[a]
ins(ere, erit) — insert, it inserts Gn 1, 7[a-a]
inserti, orum — inserted Jer 39, 13[a]
insolite — unusually Da 4, 27[a]
intenta — intended Ez 48, 2-7[a-a]
inter — between, among Nu 22, 5[c]
interpretatio — interpretation Jer 46, 2[a]
interrogativum — interrogative Dt 20, 19[b]
interv(allum) — interval Gn 4, 8[a]
intransitivum — intransitive Da 9, 1[a]
introducens, entis — introductory Da 3, 23[a]
inundationes — inundations Na 1, 12[a-a]
inusitatum — unusual Da 1, 2[a]
invenies — you will find Ex 36, 8[b]
invers — inverso ordine — in inverse order Gn 19, 28[a-a]
inverte — invert Ps 34, 16[a]
ipsi — themselves Jer 15, 11[b]
ira, ae — anger, wrath Ps 7, 14[a]
irrepsit — it crept into Da 9, 3[a]
irritator — he who irritates Ps 15, 4[b]
is, ea, ie; ii, eae, ea — he, she, it; they Jer 51, 12[a-a]
it(em) — likewise Ex 3, 8[c]
iter — way Jes 60, 4[a]
iterum — again Da 6, 2[a]
iudicium — judgment Hi 19, 29[a]
iuravi — I have taken an oath 2Ch 7, 18[a]

I I

iustificata — justified Gn 20, 16[b-b]
iuvenes, um — young men Da 3, 23[a]

J J

jdaram — judaeo-aramaicus, a, um — Jewish-Aramaic Da 4, 12[a]
judaicus, a, um — Jewish Jer 46, 2[a]
judices — judges Ex 21, 6[a]

K K

kopt(icus, a, um; e) — (in) Coptic Jes 19, 10[a]

L L

laceravi — I have torn to pieces Hi 19, 20[b]
lacuna — lacuna Ex 18, 11[a]
laetantur — they rejoice Ps 126, 1[b]
lamentationes, um — lamentations Jes 43, 14[c]
lapsus — error, lapsus calami — slip of the pen (scribal error) Ex 23, 3[a]
laquei, orum — snares, traps Ps 35, 7[b-b]
largum — plentiful Prv 13, 23[a]
latitudo — breadth, width 2Ch 3, 4[a]
lect(io) — reading Gn 18, 22[a-a]
lector, oris — reader Jer 2, 31[a-a]
legatur — let it be read 1Ch 27, 27[b]
l(ege, egendum) — read, to be read Gn 1, 11[b]
leg(ere, it, unt) — to read, it reads, they read Nu 28, 7[b]
legiones — legions Nu 24, 24[a]
legisse, legit — to have read, it has read Jer 5, 24[c]
liber, bri — book Da 1, 1[a]
libera — free (adj.) Jer 34, 5[b]
libera — release, free (verb) Ps 12, 8[b]
libere — freely Dt 5, 6[a]
licet — it is permitted Ex 19, 13[b]
lignum, i — wood Jes 40, 20[a]

L
L

locus, i — place Nu 13, 7[a-a]
locusta — locust Jes 51, 6[a-a]
longitudo, inis — length 2Ch 6, 13[b-b]
luna crescens — new moon Jes 14, 12[a]
luxa — put out of joint Nu 25, 4[c]

M
M

magi — magicians Jes 2, 6[a]
magnificus — magnificent Ex 15, 11[a]
maiestas — majesty Nu 23, 21[d]
maj(or, oris) — larger Gn 34, 31[a]
male — badly Da 4, 19[a]
maledicta — abused Jer 31, 22[b-b]
malum — evil Ps 10, 6/7[a-a]
mandatum — order Ps 17, 4[b]
mansuetus — mild, gentle Jo 4, 11[c-c]
manus, us — hand Ps 68, 32[c-c]
marg — margine — in the margin Lv 25, 22[a]
marg(inalis) — marginal 2S 11, 1[a]
margo, inis — margin Hi 9, 6[a]
m(asculinum) — masculine Nu 34, 6[c]
masculum — male Ex 13, 13[a]
mavis — you prefer Prv 13, 4[a]
m cs — metri causaā — on account of the metre Dt 32, 9[c]
me — me Jer 31, 19[a]
mediator — mediator, intercessor Hi 16, 20[a-a]
meditatur — he thinks upon Ps 10, 6/7[a-a]
melior — better 1R 7, 18[d-d]
melius — better Dt 32, 18[b]
mendacium, ii — lie Ps 139, 24[a]
mendax — lying Ps 15, 3[a]
mendosus — incorrect Esr 1, 11[a-a]
mensa, ae — table 2S 9, 11[c]
mensis, is — month Jos 5, 10[b]

M
M

meritum — reward Ps 119, 56[a]
Messias, ae — Messiah Nu 24, 17[e]
metatheticum — postpositive Jos 10, 24[e]
metropolis, eos — capital Nu 22, 39[b-b]
metrum — metre Na 3, 17[b-b]
meus, a, um — my Jer 31, 19[a]
ministerium — service Ps 26, 8[b]
ministraverunt — they have worshiped Ex 32, 35[a]
min(or) — smaller Gn 2, 25[a]
misit — he has sent 1R 5, 15[c]
mixtus, a, um — mixed Ez 9, 8[b]
mlt — multi, ae, a — many Gn 2, 18[a]
momordi — I have bitten Hi 19, 20[b]
mors, tis — death Jer 11, 19[b]
morus — mulberry tree Jes 40, 20[a]
mtr — metrum, i — metre Ez 31, 5[a-a]
mugire — to low, to bellow Jer 31, 39[d]
mulier — wife, woman Lv 18, 21[b]
munus — gift, bribe 1R 13, 33[b-b]
murus — wall Ps 122, 3[c]
mutanda, atum, atur —to be changed, changed, it is changed Esr 1, 9[b]
mutilatus, a, um — mutilated Mi 1, 10[a]

N
N

Nabataeenses — Nabataean Da 4, 13[a]
nab(ataeus, a, um; e) — (in) Nabataean Dt 33, 3[a-a]
narratum — told 1R 11, 19[a-a]
navis — ship Jes 2, 16[a]
ne — lest Ps 60, 6[c]
necavi — I have slain Neh 13, 15[a]
nectunt — they weave Jer 5, 26[a-a]
nefarii — nefarious, impious Ps 119, 23[a]
neglecto — without regard to Da 3, 17[a]

N N

neohb — neohebraicus, a, um — modern Hebrew Hi 18, 3[a]
nequaquam — not at all Da 9, 13[a]
neutrum — neuter Hi 31, 11[a]
niger — black Hi 3, 5[a]
nil — nothing Jer 5, 24[c]
nisi — unless, but Jer 5, 24[c]
nobiles — highborn, superior Jes 43, 14[a]
noluerit — he is unwilling 1Ch 28, 7[a-a]
nom(en, inis) — name Jos 15, 25[a]
non — not Ex 23, 5[a-a]
nona, ae — ninth Esr 9, 4[b-b]
nonn(ulli, ae, a) — some, several Gn 1, 30[a]
nostrum — our Esr 4, 14[a]
nota — note 2S 11, 1[a]
notum — known Hi 33, 27[a]
novum — new Ps 115, 12[a]
nubes — cloud(s) Nu 23, 10[c-c]
nullus, ius — not any Hi 10, 22[b-b]
num — (interrogative particle) Ex 2, 25[a]
numerus, i — number Ex 36, 8[b]
nunc — now Hi 9, 6[a]
nuntius, ii — messenger Nu 22, 18[a]

O O

obducti, orum — covered Ps 68, 31[b]
ob(elus, i) — obelus Dt 4, 22[a]
objectum — object Hi 17, 6[a]
oblitus est — he has forgotten Jes 44, 9[a]
obscure — darkly Ex 23, 5[a-a]
observatio — observation Qoh 3, 17[a]
obsistere — to resist, to oppose Hi 38, 11[a-a]
obturare — to block up Hi 18, 3[a]
offerebat — he brought before 1R 13, 33[b-b]
omisso — with omission of Est 9, 29[a-a]

O

O

om(ittit, unt) — it omits, they omit Gn 10, 4[a]
omnis, e — all, every Hi 10, 8[a-a]
operati sunt — they have worked Ps 73, 7[b]
operuerunt — they have covered Ps 55, 5[a]
oppositum — opposite Da 4, 5[a]
oratio, onis — prayer Da 3, 23[a]
ordinant, at — they arrange, it arranges Ex 20, 13[a]
ordo, inis — order Nu 36, 11[a]
orig(inalis) — original Gn 18, 22[a-a]
orig(inaliter) — originally Gn 4, 7[b-b]
ortus, a, um — arisen Ez 40, 14[a]

P

P

paenituit me — I have repented Jer 31, 19[a]
paenultima, ae — the penultimate (syllable) Lv 18, 28[a]
papyrus, i — papyrus Da 3, 6[c]
par(allelismus, i) — parallelism Dt 33, 13[b]
pars, tis — part Ps 35, 3[a]
particula, ae — particle 1S 2, 27[a]
partim — partly, in part Ex 36, 8[b]
partitivum — partitive Da 11, 7[b-b]
pascuum, i — pasture Jer 6, 2[a-a]
passim — here and there Jer 2, 33[b]
pass(ivum) — passive Gn 45, 2[a]
patronymicum — patronymic Nu 13, 7[a-a]
paululum — a little bit, trifle Jes 57, 17[b]
paulum — a little, somewhat Jer 49, 34[a]
pavor — fear Ps 55, 5[a]
pc — pauci, ae, a — a few Gn 1, 11[b]
pellis, is — skin, hide Neh 3, 15[d]
perdiderunt — they have destroyed Ps 35, 12[a]
perduces — you will bring through Ps 49, 20[a]
perfectus — perfect Hi 10, 8[a-a]
periphrasis, eos — circumlocution Ex 14, 20[a-a]

P P

permlt — permulti, ae, a — very many 1S 2, 10[c]
pertinens, pertinet — belonging to, it belongs to Neh 13, 28[a]
perturbatus, i — disturbed, disordered Dt 26, 17[a]
pessum data — destroyed Na 3, 11[b]
petent — they will ask, they will desire Ps 18, 42[b-b]
pf — perfectum — perfect Lv 18, 28[a]
phoneticum — phonetic Hi 36, 27[b]
pinguis — fat Hi 33, 25[a]
plaga — blow, stroke Ps 39, 11[a]
plerumque — generally Dt 31, 16[c]
pl(uralis) — plural Gn 13, 18[a]
plur(es, a) — many Jos 19, 47[c]
poetica — poetical Hi 37, 12[c]
populus, i — people Jer 33, 13[a-a]
porta — gate Da 8, 2[c-c]
possessio — possession Hi 15, 29[a]
post — after Gn 14, 1[d-d]
postea — thereafter Gn 47, 5[a]
postquam — after Cant 4, 6[a]
potens, entis — mighty Dt 32, 15[f]
potius — rather, preferably Gn 48, 20[b]
praebent, praebet — they present, it presents Ex 36, 8[b]
praecedens — preceding Mal 2, 15[c]
praecones — heralds Ex 36, 6[a-a]
praedicabit — he will praise Ps 22, 9[a]
pr(aemitte, mittendum, mittit, mittunt) — put before, to be put before, it puts before, they put before Gn 1, 30[a]
praepos(itio, onis) — preposition 2S 3, 27[c]
praeter — except Nu 22, 22[c]
praeterea — besides Ex 29, 20[a]
prb — probabiliter — probably Jer 2, 16[b]
primogenitum — first-born Ex 13, 13[a]
primus, a, um — first 1Ch 7, 15[c]

P P

princeps, ipis — chief Nu 24, 17[e]
pro — for, instead of Gn 11, 31[c]
probavit — he has tested, he has tried Jes 66, 16[b]
proclamaverunt — they have cried out Ex 36, 6[a-a]
procurrens — jutting out Hi 39, 8[a]
pron(omen) — pronoun 1S 1, 17[a]
propago, inis — shoot Ps 80, 16[a]
proprius, a, um — proper Ex 2, 1[a]
propter — because of Nu 5, 26[b-b]
propterea — therefore Da 7, 15[a-a]
prosperitas, atis — prosperity Hi 20, 20[a-a]
protectio, onis — protection Ps 42, 5[a-a]
prp — propositum — it has been proposed Jes 26, 11[a]
prs — personalis, e — personal 1S 1, 17[a]
pt — participium — participle 1S 14, 26[a]
pudicitia, ae — decency Nu 31, 18[a]
pulchra — beautiful Nu 12, 1[a]
pulvis, eris — dust Nu 23, 10[c-c]
punct(um, i) — point(s) Gn 16, 5[a]
pun(icus, a, um) — Punic Da 7, 17[a]
purus — pure Prv 26, 28[b]

Q Q

quam — than Hi 4, 19[a]
quamvis — although Dt 29, 4[c-c]
quasi — as if, just as Jer 5, 26[a-a]
quattuor — four Ez 5, 12[a]
qui, quae, quod; qui, quae, quae — who, which Nu 13, 7[a-a]
quoad — as to, as far as 1Ch 27, 4[b-b]
quocum — with whom Hi 16, 20[a-a]
quoties — how often Hi 7, 4[b]

R R

radius — beam, ray Jer 23, 5[b]
rasura — erasure Ex 36, 29[b]

R R

rebellaverunt — they have rebelled Nu 31, 16[b-b]
recte — correctly Gn 31, 46[a]
rectius — more correctly Jer 4, 20[a]
rectus, a, um — correct Ez 32, 6[a]
redii — I have returned Da 4, 33[d]
redime — redeem Ps 12, 8[b]
regalis — royal, regal Hi 12, 18[a]
regens — transitive; subject Ez 43, 7[a]; Hi 31, 18[a]
regulariter — regularly Da 5, 27[a]
relat(ivum) — relative 1S 14, 21[a]
rel(iqui, ae, a) — remaining Jdc 14, 2[d]
reliquum, i — rest Jes 9, 6[a]
removeris — you have removed Ps 22, 2[b-b]
repens — creeping Jer 46, 22[a-a]
repetitus, a, um — repeated Nu 25, 8[a-a]
res, rerum — things Gn 20, 16[b-b]
restare — to stand firm Prv 11, 7[f]
rete — net Jer 5, 26[a-a]
retento — retained Jer 18, 14[b]
rex, regis — king Jos 15, 9[a-a]
robur — strength Jes 54, 8[a]
Romani, orum — Romans Nu 24, 24[b-b]
rufi — reddish Sach 6, 6,[a-a]
rursus — again Jer 31, 19[a]

S S

saepe — often Ex 21, 28[b]
saepius — more often Jos 10, 24[e]
saginati — fattened Ps 37, 20[a-a]
sagitta, ae — arrow Ps 64, 4[a]
sagittarius — bowman Prv 26, 10[b]
sal — salt Esr 4, 14[a]
salus, utis — salvation Ps 22, 2[b-b]
sam(aritanus, a, um) — Samaritan Jos 17, 7[b]

S S

sanctificate — sanctify, make holy 2Ch 35, 3[b]
satiabor — I will be sated Ps 16, 11[a]
satiatus — sated Hi 10, 15[a]
saxetum, i — rocky area Nu 20, 19[a]
saxum — rock Hi 39, 8[a]
scandendum — to be read aloud Jo 2, 9[a]
sciatis — you know Hi 19, 29[a]
scil(icet) — namely Gn 27, 40[a]
scribendum — to be written Prv 22, 17[b-b]
scriptor, oris — writer, scribe Hi 26, 12[a]
se — himself, itself Jer 33, 13[a-a]
sec(undum) — according to Jer 4, 20[a]
secundus, a, um — second Ez 8, 3[d-d]
sed — but Gn 22, 14[a]
semel — once, a single time Jos 2, 1[e]
semper — always Gn 13, 18[a]
senior — elder 1S 19, 20[b]
sensus, us — meaning Jer 10, 5[a-a]
sententia — opinion Jes 44, 28[a]
septies — seven times Jos 2, 1[e]
sepulchrum — sepulcher, grave Jes 53, 9[c]
sepultra — burial 2Ch 26, 23[b]
sequitur — it follows 2Ch 25, 23[a-a]
sera — bar (for fastening doors) 1Ch 12, 16[b]
serpens — snake Jer 46, 22[a-a]
seu — or Gn 38, 29[a]
sexta, ae — sixth 2S 24, 15[b-b]
sg — singularis — singular Gn 7, 13[a]
si — if Ex 23, 5[a-a]
sic — so, thus Gn 2, 18[a]
silex — flint Jer 18, 14[b]
sim(ilis, e) — similar Gn 11, 11[a]
simillima — very similar 1Ch 28, 20[b]

S

S

sine — without Gn 26, 1[a]
sive — or Ex 16, 32[b]
sol(um) — only Nu 16, 24[a-a]
solus — alone, only Dt 32, 50[b]
sordes — dirt, filth Prv 10, 20[b]
soror — sister 1Ch 2, 25[b]
sors — lot Prv 12, 9[a]
sperabunt, sperate — they will hope, hope Ps 52, 8[b-b]
spes, ei — hope Ps 55, 23[a]
splendor, oris — splendor, brilliance Jer 23, 5[b]
sq — sequens — following Ex 8, 12[c]
sqq — sequentes — following Nu 3, 12[b]
statim — immediately Hi 18, 8[a]
stat(us) — state 1S 12, 23[b]
stella crinita — comet Nu 24, 17[e]
stercilinium — dunghill Na 1, 14[c-c]
stich(us) — stich Jdc 5, 11[c]
stillare — to drop, to drip Hi 36, 27[a-a]
stropha — strophe Na 1, 4[b]
studium — zeal Prv 19, 2[b]
sub — under, beneath Ex 36, 8[b]
subj(ectum) — subject 1S 20, 33[b]
subsellia — seats 2Ch 9, 11[a]
subst(antivum) — substantive, noun 2S 19, 43[b]
suff(ixum) — suffix Gn 7, 13[a]
sum — I am Ps 88, 9[b]
sumite — take Ex 12, 21[b-b]
summarium, ii — summary Da 5, 25[a]
sunt — they are Mi 1, 10[a]
super — above Ps 56, 3[c-c]
superesse — to be left Na 3, 14[b]
supervacaneus — needless, superfluous Da 10, 13[a-a]

S S

supra — above Jes 54, 13[a]
suspensum — raised Jdc 18, 30[a]
suus, a, um — his Ps 33, 17[a]
syr(iacus, a, um; e) — (in) Syriac Jer 10, 5[a-a]

T T

tacuerit, tacui — it was silent, I have been silent Ex 19, 13[a-a]
talpa — mole Ps 58, 9[b]
tantum — only Nu 8, 16[a-a]
tarditas — tardiness, slowness Prv 29, 11[a]
taurus — Taurus (astronomy) Am 5, 9[c]
te — you Ps 16, 2/3[b-b]
technicus — technical Ez 41, 6[c]
tegere — to cover Hi 23, 9[a]
tegimen — covering, cover Na 2, 4[a-a]
tegmentum, i — covering, cover Hi 23, 9[a]
templum, i — temple 2Ch 7, 9[a]
ter — thrice Jo 1, 15[a]
terminus — term Ez 41, 6[c]
terra — land Nu 22, 5[c]
tertius, ii — third Ez 40, 7/8/9[b]
testiculati — having their testicles Jer 5, 8[b]
testis, is — witness Lv 18, 11[a]
tetragrammaton — Tetragrammaton 2S 2, 27[a]
textor — weaver Jes 19, 10[a]
textus, us — text Mi 5, 4[b-b]
threnus, i — lamentation Ez 32, 18[c]
tibi — to you Dt 6, 3[d]
titulus — title Prv 22, 17[b-b]
tonitrus — thunder Jes 33, 3[a]
tot(us, a, um) — the whole Dt 9, 1[a]
tradit — it renders, translates Dt 5, 6[a]
traditio — tradition Jes 52, 14[c]

T T

transcendere — to transcend Hi 39, 8[a]
transciptio, onis — transcription, transliteration 2Ch 22, 1[a]
transl(atio) — translation Hab 3, 2[a]
tr(anspone) — transpose Gn 1, 6[a]
tu — you Gn 20, 16[b-b]
tum — then, in that case Lv 17, 4[d-d]
tumultuati sunt — they have made a tumult Da 6, 16[b]
tumultuose — tumultuously Da 6, 7[a]
tunc — then Jo 2, 9[a]
turma, ae — division 1Ch 27, 4[b-b]
tuus, a, um — your Ps 17, 15[b]
txt — textus — text Dt 33, 2[c]

U U

ubi — where Esr 8, 16[c-c]
ubique — everywhere Nu 2, 6[a]
ug(ariticus, a, um; e) — (in) Ugaritic Dt 1, 44[b]
ulciscendo — taking vengeance Hos 9, 12[a]
ultima — last Nu 36, 11[a]
ululatus — howling, wailing Jer 4, 31[b]
umbra, ae — shadow Ps 31, 21[c]
una c(um) — together with 1R 9, 16[a]
unde — wherefore Ez 28, 13[c-c]
unus, a, um — one Da 11, 7[b-b]
urbs, urbis — town, city Jer 39, 3[b-b]
urentes — burning Nu 21, 6[a]
usque ad — (right) up to Ex 36, 8[b]
ut — as; so that Gn 6, 20b; Hi 19, 29[a]
uter, tris — leather bottle Ps 33, 7[a]
utrumque — both, each Na 1, 10/11[c-c]

V V

vadum, i — ford Nu 21, 11[a]
valde — very much Da 3, 31[a]
vallis — valley Ps 84, 7[b]

V V

var(ia; varia lectio) — variant; variant reading 1R 7, 18[d-d]
vasa — vessels Hi 21, 24[a]
vb — verbum, i; verba, orum — word(s) Ex 2, 25[a]
vel — or Gn 1, 1[a]
venenum — poison Jer 11, 19[b]
venerunt, veniet — they have come, it will come Da 6, 7[a]
verba — words Lv 10, 18[a]
verbatim — literally Jos 16, 10[a]
verbatio — chastisement Hi 36, 18[b]
verbotenus — literally Nu 10, 11[a]
verb(um) — verb 1S 1, 6[a]
vere — verily, indeed Hi 6, 13[a]
veritas, atis — truth Ps 7, 12[aa]
vers(io, onis) — version, translation Esr 2, 48[a]
v(ersus) — verse Lv 24, 2[a]
versus, uum — verses Jer 19, 2[a-a]
vertit — it translates Dt 8, 13[a]
vertunt — they translate, they change Nu 12, 1[b-b]; Jer 5, 10[b-b]
vestimenta, orum — garments Da 3, 21[a-a]
vestis — garment 2R 23, 7[b]
vetus — old Nu 28, 7[b]
vexant — they torment Hi 6, 4[a]
via — way Ps 2, 11/12[c]
vide, videns — see, seeing Jer 38, 28[a]; Hi 10, 15[a]
vid(entur, etur) — they seem, it seems Gn 10, 4[b]
vindemiator — Vindemiator (astronomy) Am 5, 9[e]
vindex — liberator Ps 4, 2[b]
vinum — wine Nu 28, 7[b]
vita, ae — life Ps 143, 10[c]
vivum — alive 2Ch 33, 11[a]
vix — hardly, scarcely Hos 6, 5[d]
vobis — to you Ex 19, 13[b]

V V

vocales — vowels 1Ch 11, 22[b]
vocativus — vocative Ps 113, 1[a]
vos — yourselves 2Ch 35, 3[b]
vox — word 2S 8, 7[b]
vrb — verbum — verb Jdc 5, 14[a]
vulva, ae — womb Ex 13, 13[a]
vv — versus, uum — verses 1R 2, 46[a]

SIGNS AND VERSIONS

Signs

+ — it adds, they add
> — is wanting in, is absent in
* — the form of the word is a probable conjecture

Manuscripts and Versions

α′ — Aquila's Greek translation of the OT
𝔄 — The Arabic version of the OT
C — The Cairo Codex of the Hebrew Prophets
ℭ — A reading of one or several Hebrew manuscripts from the Cairo Geniza
Ed, Edd — One or several editions of the Hebrew OT
𝔊 — The Septuagint
K — The Ketib
L — The Leningrad Codex of the Hebrew OT
𝔐 — The Masoretic Text of the OT
Ms, Mss — One or several medieval manuscripts of the Hebrew OT

Occ — An Occidental reading
Or — An Oriental reading
Q — The Qere
𝔔 — A reading of one or several Hebrew manuscripts from Qumran
ɯ — The Samaritan Hebrew Pentateuch
$ɯ^{T}$ — The Samaritan Targum of the Pentateuch
σ′ — Symmachus's Greek translation of the OT
𝔖 — The Syriac version of the OT
𝔗 — The Targum(s)
θ′ — Theodotion's Greek translation of the OT
𝔙 — The Vulgate

Books of the Old Testament

Gn	Ex	Lv	Nu	Dt				
Jos	Jdc	1S	2S	1R	2R			
Jes	Jer	Ez	Hos	Jo	Am	Ob	Jon	Mi
		Na	Hab	Zeph	Hag	Sach	Mal	
Ps	Hi	Prv	Ru	Cant	Qoh	Thr	Est	Da
		Esr	Neh	1Ch	2Ch			

Apocrypha/Deuterocanonicals and Pseudepigrapha

Est apokr Makk Sir Jub

Books of the New Testament

Mt	Mc	Lc	J	Act				
Rm	1Ko	2Ko	G	E	Ph	Kol	1Th	2Th
	1T	2T	Tt	Phm	Hbr	Jc	1P	2P
	1J	2J	3J	Jd	Apc			

For all other symbols, consult Sigla et Compendia in the Prolegomena to *Biblia Hebraica Stuttgartensia*.